WEST BENGAL
PANCHAYAT ELECTIONS 1993

West Bengal Panchayat Elections 1993

A Study in Participation

Girish Kumar
Buddhadeb Ghosh

INSTITUTE OF SOCIAL SCIENCES
and
CONCEPT PUBLISHING COMPANY

ISBN 81-7022-539-6

First Published in 1996

Published and Printed by
Ashok Kumar Mittal
Concept Publishing Company
A/15-16, Commercial Block, Mohan Garden
NEW DELHI 110 059 (India)

Layout by
Institute of Social Sciences
B-7/18 Safdarjung Enclave
New Delhi 110 029

Contents

Foreword

The present study is the latest in the series on Panchayati Raj by the Institute of Social Sciences. It is part of our major project: "Present Status and Future Prospects of Panchayati Raj" covering eight states, including West Bengal. The Institute launched this project in the second half of 1992; few months prior to the Parliament passing the 73rd Constitution Amendment. The West Bengal government had announced panchayat elections for May 1993 even before the Constitution Amendment was published in the Gazette of India and the existing state Panchayat Act amended. The 1993 May election was considered a valuable opportunity to look into several aspects of panchayati raj because panchayati raj in West Bengal had achieved a distinct place in the country's post-independent history of grassroots democracy, local government and rural development.

West Bengal was the first state to revive panchayati raj following the Asoka Mehta Committee's recommendations in 1978. Since then it was the only state which had conducted elections every five years without fail. While in states such as Andhra Pradesh, Karnataka and Kerala, the second generation panchayats could not survive following the defeat of the non-Congress parties in power, in West Bengal, the panchayat system had not only survived but has also carved a niche for itself for introducing many innovations in the field. Several studies including that of G.K. Lieten, Kirsten Westergaard and Neil Webster testify to this fact.

Dr. Girish Kumar, coordinator of the project at the Institute, in co-operation with Mr. Buddhadeb Ghosh, the then Director of the Kalyani (Nadia)-based State Institute of Panchayats, Government of West Bengal, presently with the Institute, took up the study. The election period proved to be an ideal time to observe the extent of people's participation in panchayats in general and elections in particular. The survey was carried out in the month of May-June 1993 i.e., before and after the panchayat elections in four selected panchayat areas. Supplementary information was also gathered during their subsequent field visits.

The authors have gone well beyond just the questions of election process and voting behaviour. They conclude that apart from implementing rural development programmes efficiently in the villages, the political panchayats are credited with performing even those functions which are not assigned to them, such as settlement of village disputes, etc. On the other hand, according to the study, the panchayats do not seem to be encouraging people sufficiently, to involve themselves in development programmes.

New insights which this study gives in the understanding of the panchayat system in West Bengal, I hope, will help future research on the subject.

New Delhi
December 1995

George Mathew
Director

Acknowledgements

Mr Partha Sarathi De, Mr Partha Das, Mr Shankar Prasad Sikdar and Mr Sushant Kumar Banerjee carried out the field work for this study during the months of May-June, 1993. Mr Ratan Ghosh, a former District Panchayat Officer took care of logistics and also accompanied us during our field visits. We wish to thank all of them. A word of special thanks is also due to Mr Arabindo Ghosh, a senior faculty member of the State Institute of Panchayats (SIP), Kalyani, for supervising the tabulation work.

In the course of this study we received co-operation from many quarters: from the officials of the Directorate of Panchayats, Government of West Bengal, Calcutta and SIP, Kalyani; from the leaders of different political parties and front organizations of the CPI(M), particularly, from pradhans and secretaries of several Gram Panchayats as well as from the common people in many villages. Space does not permit us to name each and everyone but we wish to record our gratitude to all of them.

We also owe a word of special appreciation to Ms. Priti Anand and Mr. Vivek Kaushik for their editorial comments. Last but not least, we are grateful to Mr Nirmal Mukarji, former cabinet secretary and former Governor of Punjab, who took pains to go through the earlier draft. We wish to put it on record that we were immensely benefitted by his comments and suggestions. However, we are solely responsible for any error or logical inadequacies that may still remain.

We also wish to thank Mr. P. Nand Kumar and Ms. Sapna Sharma for corrections and revisions, and Mr. P. N. Kuttappan for the layout of this book.

New Delhi
1995

Girish Kumar
Buddhadeb Ghosh

Part One

Chapter I

Introduction

An Overview of West Bengal Panchayats

West Bengal can claim distinction for facilitating healthy growth of its Panchayati Raj Institutions. Firstly, these institutions have been allowed to flourish without interruption since 1978, whereas in those states which introduced panchayati raj following the report of the Asoka Mehta Committee (1978), indiscriminate suppression of elected bodies seriously jeopardised its growth. Secondly, elections to the panchayat bodies have been held at regular intervals of five years – a feat achieved, apart from West Bengal, only by the state of Gujarat among all the states of the country. Thirdly, West Bengal was a pioneer in introducing direct elections to all the three tiers of the Panchayati Raj Institutions to make the representatives of elected bodies directly responsible to the people. Fourthly, the panchayats have been given substantial funds and power to implement rural development schemes or programmes sponsored by the state or central government. This decentralisation policy has enabled the panchayat to emerge as an institution of importance and to demonstrate to the people its usefulness. Last but not the least, West Bengal introduced for the first time in the country the concept of 'Political Panchayats' enabling the political parties to participate in the elections to these bodies, thus putting an end to the controversy over partyless democracy for rural areas.

The genesis of the present panchayati raj system in the state is the spectacular electoral victory in 1977 of the Front consisting of Left parties, particularly the Communist Party of India (Marxist). The latter alone won 177 of the 294 Legislative Assembly seats, thus establishing its political supremacy in the state. Immediately after assumption of office, the new government focused its attention on the agrarian sector and launched a programme of land reform. The reform envisaged was not of any radical type, but one of strict application of laws enacted within the framework of the Constitution. As stated by the then Land Reform Commissioner, its objectives were: (i) Identification and vesting of ceiling-surplus land; (ii) distribution of vested land to the landless; (iii) registration of sharecroppers through a massive drive which came to be known as 'Operation Barga' and (iv) providing non-land inputs to the beneficiaries of land reform.[1]

Earlier, in 1967-70, West Bengal witnessed mass movements against big landowners for unearthing ceiling-surplus lands illegally held by them. These movements received direct patronage of the first and the second United Front governments and they not only politicised the rural areas, but also succeeded in unearthing huge amounts of ceiling surplus land. All these 'considerably weakened the hold of big landlords who had traditionally led rural society because of their dominant economic and social position'.[2] The spectacular win of the Left parties in 1977 also demoralised them. A new class in rural areas, mostly comprising middle and small peasantry, petty traders, professionals (overwhelmingly teachers), etc., was waiting to assert its rights. The situation offered a unique opportunity for the new Left Front government to introduce panchayats, for, chances of these institutions being taken over by the traditional power-elite, were minimal.

A legislation providing for a three-tier local government had been passed by the previous Congress government in 1973 but was never implemented. The new Left Front government amended the then existing act substantially and declared elections in June 1978 to usher in the first political panchayat in the country.

Incidentally, the period 1977-78 also witnessed a major turning point in the history of panchayati raj in India. In 1977, for the first time a non-Congress government, basically a coalition government led by the Janata Party, had come to power in New Delhi. The new government constituted a committee, headed by Asoka Mehta to review and evaluate the working of Panchayati Raj Institutions in India. In contrast to the views held by many, including the Balwantray Mehta Study Team (1957), the Asoka Mehta Committee strongly advocated participation of political parties in Panchayati Raj Institutions. Another notable recommendation of this Committee was for the setting up of two-tier panchayat system in the states – District Panchayats and Mandal Panchayats.* Besides, the Committee had also argued for the need for decentralisation of power below the state level, the Committee also argued for the constitutional recognition of panchayats as well as reconsideration of distribution of power between the Union and the States. This report, submitted in August 1978, generated substantial enthusiasm for reviving moribund panchayat institutions and gave birth to what is known as second generation panchayats in states like Karnataka, Andhra Pradesh and Kerala.

The launching of panchayati raj in West Bengal was preceded by mass movements for altering the land-owning pattern in the countryside (1967-1970), and was accompanied by concerted administrative action for land reform, particularly with respect to the vesting/distribution of ceiling-surplus land and ensuring security of tenure of sharecroppers (1977-1982). The point that needs emphasis is that panchayati raj in the state was not conceived in a vacuum, divorced from rural society, which by no means is homogeneous and where the traditional power structure, represented by the landed gentry, has the capacity to hijack even a democratic system. The uniqueness of West Bengal panchayat system lies in the fact that it has brought into focus the issue of land reform in the creation of panchayati raj, so that the panchayat institutions do not turn out to be hunting grounds of rural elite. Accordingly, it has been claimed by the Left Front government that land reform is inseparable from democratic decentralisation and the two together are the "two legs" of the rural development programme of the state.[3]

To what extent has this two-leg policy been carried to its logical end and to what measure it has succeeded in empowering the poor and the under-privileged through their active participation in the panchayat system are questions that demand deeper probe. But the fact remains that by asserting that the policy of democratic decentralisation will be devoid of substance unless the power base of traditional rural elite is

---

*Mandal Panchayat: Comprising a group of villages with a population of 19-20,000. Once fully operational, it would replace both GP and PS.

weakened, the issues have been sufficiently politicised. Credit should go to the Left Front government of West Bengal, at least, for linking the issue of land reform with that of panchayati raj.

The panchayats of West Bengal, today, are busy centres of activity; an account of the various activities now being performed by all the tiers of the panchayat system will not be feasible due to lack of space. Suffice it to say, for the present, that there is hardly any rural development activity in the state in which panchayats are not involved directly or indirectly. Thanks to the holding of regular elections, panchayats have paved the way for the emergence of thousands of public figures many of whom have shown considerable promise as leaders. If not for anything else, this in itself has been a positive contribution of the West Bengal panchayat system in strengthening democracy.

Background

For more than a decade and a half, West Bengal has been in the forefront of the panchayati raj movement. In 1993, the state's panchayat institutions completed their third five-year term and the fourth general election was fixed for 30 May of that year. This election was notable for two reasons. Firstly, the notification fixing the date and time of poll was issued at a time (10 March 1993), when the historic 73rd Constitution Amendment, after being passed in the Parliament, was awaiting ratification by states and the President's assent. Thus the election was to be held in the backdrop of an imminent change in the administrative set-up of the country, for panchayat would henceforth be a constitutional entity endowed with substantial state functions. Secondly, the election was preceded by amendments in the state's Panchayat Act which, *inter alia*, provided, for the first time, reservation of seats for women, Scheduled Castes and Scheduled Tribes. Anticipating a constitutional amendment, not less than one-third of the seats in all the tiers were reserved for women, and for SC/STs, seats were reserved in accordance with the proportion of such population to the total population. Therefore this was the first panchayat election in the country where reservation provisions as visualised in the 73rd Constitution Amendment were applied, although the election was not being held strictly as per the terms of this amendment, as the notification was issued before the same came into force. Of the 71,113 seats in the three tiers, more than 42,000 seats (fifty-five per cent) were reserved seats, 24,855 seats (thirty-five per cent) being reserved for women[4], including SC/ST women. The reservation threw up a new situation. The political parties had to locate suitable candidates for reserved seats especially for women. Most of the candidates for these seats would be freshers in the arena of politics and for the voters, it was going to be a novel experience to see such a large number of women and members of SC/ST contesting for panchayat seats.

Thus on the eve of the 1993 election, the mature panchayat bodies of West Bengal, with fifteen years' experience behind them, were entering into a new phase. We felt that this election would provide us with an opportunity to gain new insights on the institutionalisation of panchayats and people's attitude towards this local level institution.

Objectives

Even though the election prompted us to undertake the study, this is not a work on electoral politics nor is it a typical study on voting behaviour. Utilising the occasion, we have tried to assess the extent and the nature of institutionalisation of panchayat system in West Bengal. More specifically, our objectives have been to gain insight into the following:

- The extent to which the panchayats have taken root in rural West Bengal;
- The attitude of people towards these institutions;
- The extent of participation of people in the activities of panchayats;
- The attitude of people towards panchayat elections and the manner in which they perform their role as electors.

It is worthwhile to mention that the first panchayat election of West Bengal (1978), was studied by M. Shivaiah and others.[5] This was in the nature of a benchmark survey of peoples' response to the launching of a new generation of panchayats, all the tiers of which would be directly elected, elections being fought openly, for the first time, by the political parties. It was an election for building new institutions almost from scratch. The above-mentioned study tried to capture this initial process of institution-building. In contrast to this, we utilised the fourth election (1993) to form an idea of the nature and the depth of institutionalisation of panchayats in the course of the last fifteen years.

Conceptual Framework

It is through institutions that the State establishes its linkage with society. Such linkage enables the State to extend its fiat to the people. It also enables people to make demands upon the State as well as to influence governmental decisions that affect them. Since a democratic State is based on the consent of the people, the latter's interaction with political institutions assume importance in democracy. In other words, to have institutions alone is not enough. In order to make it appropriate for a democratic State, it has to acquire legitimacy in the minds of the people. 'Whereas institutionalization provides the mechanical and structural contact between the State and society, legitimation links the two emotionally and psychologically.'[6]

In India, bureaucracy has remained one of the most crucial State institutions. It was the main apparatus of imperialist rule and its role increased in the post-independence period. In course of time, it expanded manifold to act as the major forum of contact between the masses and the government and as the principal agent for implementing welfare and developmental goals of the democratic State. The inadequacy of the bureaucracy to perform these twin roles became apparent, as soon as the democratic aspirations and political consciousness of the people began to grow.

On the one hand, the field-level bureaucracy at the village, block or district levels, responsible as it is only to itself, was found to be hopelessly inadequate to act as a forum for channelising peoples' demands and aspirations into the political system. On the other hand, as the State began to penetrate more and more into rural society with welfare and development programmes in various sectors, it became apparent soon that the bureaucracy was not equipped to handle programmes which require involvement and participation of people for their success. Thus in the context of growing consciousness of the people and ever-increasing volume of social and economic development programmes of the state, the field-level bureaucracy as representative of the State, not being subject to any kind of popular control at the local level, appears to have lost its effectiveness as well as legitimacy. For certain kinds of rural development programmes, it is an imperfect delivery system. As a point of contact between the masses and the government, it has no value, since, by its very nature, the bureaucracy does not allow any space for political input and participation. This institution is thus unable to bridge the gap between State and society.

The importance of the panchayat system in the democratic governance of our country has to be understood in this context. Following the lead given by the Balwantray Mehta Committee, there is a tendency to view the panchayat institutions principally as an instrument for implementing certain rural development programmes conceived at the levels of state or central governments. No doubt, being a popular institution, its capacity to involve and mobilise people around a development programme cannot be equalled by the bureaucracy. But this instrumental value of panchayat does not capture its full significance. As an institution, the panchayat is capable of performing a much bigger role. Operating at the local level, it shares State power and, as such, it is the government for the local area, capable of reflecting 'local will' as distinct from the will of the State expressed through higher level governments. Being a popular institution operating in a very small area, it can allow space for participation of people in its affairs. People also find it easier to participate, since the institution functions right in front of their eyes and their activities are transparent. By allowing the 'local will' to find an expression through extensive participation of people, the panchayat has the capability, more than any other institution, to close the gap between the State and society. It is here that the real significance of institutionalization of the panchayat lies. To view the institution as a mere instrument of higher level government, is to underestimate its potential. The panchayat is capable of fulfilling a vital institutional gap in India's democratic polity, if it is allowed to emerge as an institution of self-government for the local area. Such conceptualization of panchayati raj has guided this study.

Methodology

In formulating our view, we have basically relied on primary data for which a structured questionnaire was canvassed to 1,190 villagers distributed over four Gram Panchayat areas situated in four districts, viz., 24-Parganas (South), Nadia, Burdwan and Maldah. In each sample panchayat area, around 300 respondents selected to include people belonging to different socio-economic strata were interviewed.

The field data were supplemented by personal interviews with the leaders of political parties, panchayat leaders as well as common people. Besides, wherever necessary, we have drawn insight from secondary data.

Organisation of the Report

The study report is organized under two parts. Part One has six chapters. An overview of the West Bengal panchayat system and background of the study is given in the introductory chapter. The second chapter contains the profile of the study area and respondents. In the next three chapters (third, fourth and fifth) we have presented the survey findings. Lastly, chapter six contains our concluding remarks.

Part Two comprises chapters seven and eight. The facts and analysis presented in chapters seven and eight do not form part of our field study but these are very much relevant to the 1993 panchayat election. Chapter seven provides information on, and where necessary, analysis of, certain features of the fourth panchayat election. The chapter is divided into four sections. In the first section, data on such aspects as voter strength, reservation of seats, party-wise candidates for seats, participation of women candidates and voters' participation are presented. In the second section, special features obtaining in Darjeeling district in respect of panchayat elections are provided. The third section deals with the style of campaigning and manifestos of different political parties. Lastly, in the fourth section, an analysis of the response of the print media towards this election has been attempted.

Chapter eight contains macro-level data and performance levels of different political parties in all the four elections held so far (1978-1993).

Notes and References

1. D. Bandyopadhyay, *Land Reforms in West Bengal*, Government of West Bengal, 1980.
2. Nirmal Mukarji and D. Bandyopadhyay, *New Horizons for West Bengal Panchayats*, Government of West Bengal, 1993, p.3.
3. Surya Kanta Mishra, *An Alternative Approach to Development: Land Reforms and Panchayats*, Government of West Bengal, 1991. Also see text of his speech at the conference held at New Delhi on 9 October 1992. "In our rural development efforts", said Dr Mishra, Minister for Panchayats and Rural Development, West Bengal, at the conference, "we must depend on both the legs. One, of course, is land reforms, the other of the two being democratic decentralisation."
4. The Panchayat law of West Bengal (as well as the 73rd Constitution Amendment) provided for reservation of 'not less than one-third' of the total seats of panchayat bodies for women. If the total number of seats in a panchayat is not divisible by three, then the number of reserved seats for women becomes more than the stipulated one-third of total seats. That is why in totality, the percentage of reserved seats for women has been 35 instead of 33.33.
5. M. Shivaiah, K.B. Srivastava and A.C. Jena, *Panchayati Raj Elections in West Bengal, 1978*, NIRD, Hyderabad, 1980.
6. Mehran Kamrava, *Politics and Society in the Third World*, Routledge, 1993.

Chapter II

Profile of the Study Area and the Respondents

Study Area

Four Gram Panchayats, one each from four different districts, were selected for the study. They vary in terms of degree of development as well as organizational strength of political forces dominating the areas. The panchayats were Durgapur (Burdwan), Kasthadanga (Nadia), Baharu Kshetra (South 24-Parganas) and Sahapur (Maldah).

Durgapur panchayat is under Memari-I block of **Burdwan** district. Burdwan is the most prosperous district of West Bengal. Fed by the Damodar Valley Canal system, this district has witnessed phenomenal growth in agricultural production over the last three decades. Today, it is one of the leading producers of rice in the country. The western part of the district–which includes Asansol and Durgapur subdivisions–is highly industrialized, being the major coal-steel complex of the country. The overall impact of both industrial and agricultural development is well reflected in the female literacy rate–one of the major indicators of the social development of any given place. This is 43.61 per cent for Burdwan, the highest compared to other three selected districts.

Politically, also, this district is highly developed. Being the home district of the legendary peasant leader, Harekrishna Konar and Benoy Chowdhury, the present land reforms minister of the state, Burdwan is the stronghold of the CPI(M). In the 1988 and 1993 elections, all the seats of the Memari-I Panchayat Samiti were won by the CPI(M). All the ten Gram Panchayats in Memari-I block are controlled by the CPI(M). In Durgapur Gram Panchayat, twenty-four out of twenty-five seats were won by that party in the 1993 election. In the 1988 election, the party had won all the twenty-five seats.

Maldah district, from where **Sahapur** Gram Panchayat was selected, presents an opposite picture (a mere 20.2 per cent female literacy rate). Situated in north Bengal which has been traditionally underdeveloped compared to the southern part of the state, Maldah is virtually devoid of industries. In terms of agricultural production too, it is one of the backward districts of the state.

In Maldah the Congress party has had some influence. Being the home district of A. B. A. Ghanikhan Chowdhury, former central minister and member of Congress Working Committee, the district received benefits from several government programmes. But their impact on the overall development of the district has been less than conspicuous and possibly without any positive contribution to the organizational strength of the Congress party.

The Congress had captured the Zilla Parishad in 1983, but could not retain its hold in the subsequent election. In Sahapur, the Gram Panchayat was taken by the Congress in 1988; it won fourteen of the twenty-five seats, the remaining eleven having gone to the Left Front. In 1993, it failed to win any seat and as many as seventeen seats out of twenty-five were captured by the BJP, the remaining eight being won by the CPI(M). This Gram Panchayat is under the old Maldah block. The Panchayat Samiti of the block has been under the control of the CPI(M), both in 1988 and 1993. Out of six Gram Panchayats in this Panchayat Samiti, three are held by the CPI(M) and two by the Congress. One Gram Panchayat is now with the BJP.

South 24 Parganas district, to which **Baharu Kshetra** Gram Panchayat belongs, is economically in the middle category. A major part of this district is riverine, being situated in the deltaic Sundarbans area.

Apart from agriculture, fisheries and forestry provide employment to many in this district. A good number of people from South 24-Parganas, which borders Calcutta metropolis, are engaged in service or trade. The district has a history of peasant movements. This is the district which witnessed the famous Tebhaga peasant movement in the late forties. Even though the CPI(M) has an overwhelming influence in the district, there are areas where another Marxist party, the Socialist Unity Centre of India (SUCI) dominates. Being a bitter critic of the CPI(M), the SUCI is not part of the ruling Left Front.

Joynagar-I block, under which Baharu Kshetra Gram Panchayat falls, is one of the areas under the influence of the SUCI. Out of twelve Gram Panchayats in this block, eight have been held by the SUCI since 1988. Baharu Kshetra Gram Panchayat had been retained by the Congress both in 1988 and 1993, even though it had to make an alliance with the BJP in 1993 when the latter won two seats. Thus, this is a Gram Panchayat where the Congress holds power, even though both the CPI(M) and the SUCI have a presence in the area. Most of the areas surrounding this panchayat are under the influence of the SUCI.

The profile of **Nadia** district, from where **Kasthadanga** Gram Panchayat was chosen, is again somewhat different. Situated on the Indo-Bangladesh border, **Nadia** has seen a large influx of refugees. After resettlement in the district, the refugees have brought about substantial change in its economy specially in the field of agriculture. Today, in terms of agricultural production Nadia is one of the leading districts of the state. The district is also the traditional home of handloom and handicraft industries. Besides, Nadia holds a prominent place in the cultural history of Bengal, being the home of Chaitanya Dev, one of the greatest social and religious reformers of medieval India, and D. L. Roy (1863-1913), a famous Bengali poet. Politically also, the district is quite developed. Organizationally, the CPI(M) is the strongest party in the district, but the Congress has influence in some pockets. Of late, by inciting the issue of Bangladeshi infiltrators, the BJP has been able to make its presence felt in some areas. Additionally, there are Naxalities in some pockets, even though their impact on electoral politics has been negligible.

Coming specifically to Kasthadanga-I Gram Panchayat and Haringhata Panchayat Samiti under which the Gram Panchayat falls, the CPI(M) is the dominant party. Out of nineteen seats in Kasthadanga-I Gram Panchayat, fifteen were held by the CPI(M), two by the Forward Bloc, another Left Front party, and two by the BJP. In the earlier election, out of twenty-five seats* in this Gram Panchayat twenty-one were held by the CPI(M) and four by the Congress. In 1993, Congress could not secure any seat. So far as Haringhata Panchayat Samiti is concerned, the CPI(M) retained its authority in 1993. The hold of the

CPI(M) in the area is evident from the fact that of the ten Gram Panchayats in Haringhata block, nine are held by the party and only one by the Congress.

Socio-Economic Profile of the Respondents

While it was intended that the sample size of respondents in each of the four selected Gram Panchayats areas be 300, the actual number fell short by eight and two in Kasthadanga and Baharu panchayats respectively.

Nearly sixty per cent of the total respondents belonged to the age group of eighteen to thirty-five years (Table 2.1). Over one-fourth of the respondents were in the age group of thirty-six to fifty. Only about seven per cent respondents were in the age group of sixty and above. In Baharu Gram Panchayat, the proportion was as low as two per cent. With eighty-five per cent of respondents within the age group of eighteen to fifty, the views reflected in this study are predominantly of those active in social and economic spheres.

Seventy per cent of the respondents were male (Table 2.2), though the number of women respondents should have been larger.

A little less than one-third of the respondents were illiterate (Table 2.3). Thirty-six per cent had received education upto primary level and twenty-seven per cent upto secondary level. Only around six per cent of the respondents were graduates, while those with technical diplomas etc. constituted less than one per cent. But then this is hardly surprising, since people who receive technical education normally move to towns and cities in search of suitable jobs and better standards of living.

Unlike many states in northern India, the caste factor does not play a prominent role in the politics of West Bengal. However, leadership in social and political matters is still retained by people belonging to upper and middle castes. Besides, caste status generally, though not necessarily, reflects class position also. The incidence of poverty is more acute among the lower castes.

Twenty-nine per cent respondents belonged to the SC and ST categories and twenty-one percent were non-Hindus. Less than thirty per cent of the respondents were upper and upper middle caste persons (see Table 2.4). The sample thus had fair representation of lower caste and religious minority groups.

Table 2.1
Age Distribution of Respondents

Age	Kasthadanga	Baharu	Sahapur	Durgapur	Total
18-20	26 (8.90)	35 (11.74)	21 (7.00)	30 (10.00)	112 (9.41)
21-35	145 (49.65)	153 (51.34)	129 (43.00)	154 (51.33)	581 (48.82)
36-50	76 (26.02)	76 (25.50)	103 (34.33)	69 (23.00)	324 (27.22)
51-60	30 (10.27)	28 (9.39)	21 (7.00)	16 (5.33)	95 (7.98)
60-above	15 (5.13)	6 (2.01)	26 (8.66)	31 (10.33)	78 (6.55)
Total	292 (100.0)	298 (100.0)	300 (100.0)	300 (100.0)	1190 (100.0)

Table 2.2
Sex Composition of Respondents

	Kasthadanga	Baharu	Sahapur	Durgapur	Total
Male	185 (63.36)	249 (83.56)	220 (73.33)	175 (58.33)	829 (69.66)
Female	107 (36.64)	49 (16.44)	80 (26.67)	125 (41.67)	361 (30.34)
Total	292 (100)	298 (100)	300 (100)	300 (100)	1190 (100)

Table 2.3
Educational Status of Respondents

Educational level	Kasthadanga	Baharu	Sahapur	Durgapur	Total
Illiterate	47 (16.10)	64 (21.48)	110 (36.67)	136 (45.33)	357 (30.00)
Upto Primary	130 (44.52)	93 (31.21)	92 (30.66)	118 (39.33)	433 (36.39)
Upto Secondary	108 (36.98)	95 (31.88)	82 (27.33)	33 (11.00)	318 (26.72)
Tech.Diploma	-	5 (1.67)	3 (1.00)	-	8 (0.67)
Graduate	7 (2.40)	41 (13.75)	13 (4.33)	13 (4.33)	74 (6.22)
Total	292 (100.00)	298 (100.00)	300 (100.00)	300 (100.00)	1190 (100.00)

Table 2.4
Distribution of Respondents by Caste

Category	Kasthadanga	Baharu	Sahapur	Durgapur	Total
Upper	16 (5.48)	54 (18.12)	8 (2.67)	14 (4.67)	92 (7.73)
Middle	64 (21.92)	38 (12.75)	103 (34.33)	49 (16.33)	254 (21.34)
Lower Middle	64 (21.92)	69 (23.15)	85 (28.33)	22 (7.33)	240 (20.17)
S.C.	82 (28.08)	54 (18.12)	44 (14.67)	77 (25.67)	257 (21.60)
S.T.	2 (0.68)	1 (0.34)	22 (7.33)	67 (22.33)	92 (7.73)
Others	64 (21.92)	82 (27.51)	38 (12.67)	71 (23.67)	255 (21.43)
Total	292 (100.00)	298 (100.00)	300 (100.00)	300 (100.00)	1190 (100.00)

Table 2.5
Distribution of Respondents by Occupation

Occupation	Kasthadanga	Baharu	Sahapur	Durgapur	Total
Owner cultivator	50 (17.12)	30 (10.07)	5 (1.67)	41 (13.67)	126 (10.59)
Owner cultivator and share-cropper	27 (9.24)	26 (8.72)	18 (6.00)	4 (1.33)	75 (6.30)
Share-cropper	10 (3.42)	21 (7.04)	2 (0.67)	5 (1.67)	38 (3.19)
Patta holder	0	2 (0.67)	1 (0.33)	3 (1.00)	6 (0.50)
Patta holder and agricultural labour	4 (1.37)	2 (0.67)	8 (2.67)	10 (3.33)	24 (2.02)
Agricultural labour	23 (7.88)	46 (15.43)	9 (3.00)	114 (38.00)	192 (16.13)
Industrial worker	-	-	13 (4.33)	-	13 (1.09)
Business	26 (8.90)	42 (14.10)	36 (12.00)	13 (4.33)	117 (9.84)
Service	8 (2.73)	81 (27.19)	20 (6.67)	18 (6.00)	127 (10.68)
Others	34 (11.64)	1 (0.33)	148 (49.33)	24 (8.00)	207 (17.39)
None	110 (37.70)	47 (15.78)	40 (13.33)	68 (22.67)	265 (22.27)
Total	292 (100.00)	298	300	300	1190 (100.00)

Table 2.6
Pattern of land ownership among respondents

Land owned (in acres)	Kasthadanga	Baharu	Sahapur	Durgapur	Total
Upto 1 acre	72 (24.66)	53 (17.79)	40 (13.33)	29 (9.67)	194 (16.30)
1.00-2.5	53 (18.15)	46 (15.43)	36 (12.00)	12 (4.00)	147 (12.35)
2.5-5.00	48 (16.43)	10 (3.35)	19 (6.33)	28 (9.33)	105 (8.82)
5.0-7.5	6 (2.06)	-	8 (2.67)	20 (6.67)	34 (2.86)
7.5 and above	7 (2.40)	2 (0.68)	2 (0.67)	18 (6.00)	29 (2.44)
Landless	106 (36.30)	187 (62.75)	195 (65.00)	193 (64.33)	681 (57.23)
Total	292	298	300	300	1190 (100.00)

Occupational distribution of the respondents is shown in Table 2.5. The respondents were asked to indicate their principal occupation. It is seen that for around thirty-nine per cent of the respondents, including patta holders and agriculture labourers, agriculture is the main occupation. Another thirty-nine per cent are engaged in occupations other than agriculture, namely business, service etc. Twenty-two per cent of the respondents reported no occupation. Such an answer, however, does not necessarily indicate that the respondent is unemployed. Among such respondents were many women as well as those who do not have any viable occupation. About one-fifth of the respondents appear to be landless, because they belong to the categories of agricultural labourers and sharecroppers.

Despite all these limitations, land ownership data gives a general idea of economic and income status in rural areas (see Table 2.6). Only five per cent of the respondents owned above five acres of land. From this it can safely be concluded that the Gram Panchayat areas where the field studies were conducted are dominated by small and marginal peasants. This conforms to the general pattern of land ownership of rural West Bengal where more than seventy-five per cent of agricultural land rests with small and marginal peasants.

Notes and References

* Due to the population growth and consequent increase in number of voters this Gram Panchayat was divided into two GPs – Kasthadanga I and Kasthadanga II. The Kasthadanga I GP selected for this study had nineteen seats. Hence the change in number of seats in 1993 as compared to 1988 panchayat election.

Chapter III

Panchayats and the People

An active panchayat system has been functioning in the state for more than a decade. In May 1993, people were required to choose their panchayat representatives for the fourth time. The success of a democratic system is directly proportional to the value attached by the people to, and the interest shown by them in the functioning of the system.

To assess the extent to which the panchayat system has taken root in rural West Bengal, the respondents were asked questions relating to: (i) their awareness about panchayat institutions, (ii) their perceptions as regards the usefulness of these institutions and (iii) their assessment of the impact panchayats have made in the social, economic and political life of the villages.

Awareness About Panchayats

Two indicators were devised to measure the extent of the respondents' awareness about panchayat institutions: (i) the extent of knowledge with regard to the three-tier panchayat system; (ii) familiarity with the names of the representatives in different tiers. The results can be seen in Tables 3.1 and 3.2.

Table 3.1 shows that on an average only 10.67 per cent respondents do not have any idea about any of the three tiers of the panchayat system. While the number of such persons is higher than average in Sahapur and Durgapur (seventeen per cent each), it is insignificant in other two Gram Panchayats (five and three per cent in Kasthadanga and Baharu respectively). About forty-three per cent of the respondents have knowledge about all the three tiers, while a similar percentage of respondents have an idea about the Gram Panchayat only. That leaves about four per cent respondents who knew about two panchayat tiers. While the respondents of Baharu are most enlightened, those of Durgapur are the least where only four per cent respondents have knowledge about all the three tiers. But here also about eighty-three per cent respondents have knowledge about the Gram Panchayat.

The ordinary rural voters may not know much about institutional niceties, but with respect to a grassroots level democratic institution, it will be a sad situation if the names of the elected members of panchayats are not familiar to them.

Table 3.1
Awareness About Three-Tier Panchayat System

	Kastha-danga	Baharu	Sahapur	Durgapur	Total
Have knowledge about GP only	160 (54.79)	33 (11.07)	82 (27.33)	235 (78.33)	510 (42.86)
Have knowledge about GP and PS	5 (1.71)	7 (2.35)	16 (5.33)	-	28 (2.35)
Have knowledge about GP and ZP	16 (5.48)	-	-	-	16 (1.34)
Have knowledge of all the three tiers	96 (32.88)	249 (83.56)	151 (50.33)	13 (4.33)	509 (42.77)
Have no knowledge about any of the three tiers	15 (5.14)	9 (3.02)	51 (17.00)	52 (17.33)	127 (10.67)
Total	292 (100)	298 (100)	300 (100)	300 (100)	1190 (100)

While about ten per cent of the respondents in Kasthadanga, Sahapur and Durgapur did not know the name of even a single panchayat functionary, the number of such respondents in Baharu was nil (Table 3.2). In fact, a little less than fifty per cent of the Baharu respondents knew the names of the chairpersons and members of all three tiers, a markedly higher proportion as compared to the ten and thirteen per cent in the other Gram Panchayats. One-third of the Baharu respondents

Table 3.2
Knowledge About the Names of Panchayat Functionaries

	Kastha-danga	Baharu	Sahapur	Durgapur	Total
Know the name of pradhan only	15 (5.13)	11 (3.69)	16 (5.33)	90 (30.00)	132 (11.09)
Know the name of the local member of GP only	54 (18.50)	-	51 (17.00)	146 (48.67)	251 (21.09)
Know the name of both pradhan and GP member	109 (37.33)	43 (14.43)	107 (35.67)	-	259 (21.76)
Know the name of pradhan, sabhapati GP member and PS member	42 (14.39)	100 (33.56)	58 (19.33)	-	200 (16.80)
Know the name of the members of GP, PS and ZP as also those of pradhan, sabhapati and sabhadhipati	38 (13.01)	144 (48.32)	41 (13.67)	31 (10.33)	254 (21.34)
Know none of the names of panchayat functionaries	34 (11.64)	-	27 (9.00)	33 (11.00)	94 (7.89)
Total	292 (100)	298 (100)	300 (100)	300 (100)	1190 (100)

knew the names of the chairpersons and members of the Gram Panchayats and Panchayat Samitis, as compared to fourteen and nineteen per cent in Kasthadanga and Sahapur respectively. In Durgapur Gram Panchayat, a little less than eighty per cent of the respondents' familiarity with panchayat functionaries was limited to the Gram Panchayat level. Forty-nine per cent knew the names of Gram Panchayat member(s) only, while thirty per cent could identify only the *pradhan* (elected head of the Gram Panchayat) of their Gram Panchayat. Another ten per cent knew the names of local members of all the three tiers, leaving eleven per cent who knew none. Among the four panchayat areas, respondents of **Durgapur** seem to be least knowledgeable about the members of PRIs.

Taking Tables 3.1 and 3.2 together, we may conclude that people are reasonably aware, at least about the existence of panchayat institutions. Most of them have an idea about the Gram Panchayat and a fairly good number have knowledge about the system consisting of three tiers. The fact that ninety-two per cent of the respondents know the name of at least their local representative in the Gram Panchayat and over one-third know the name of the chairperson of their Gram Panchayat, indicates that the panchayats, at least at the lowest tier, have acquired a place of significance in the lives of the rural people.

If aware about the institutions, do the people consider them useful? What is their attitude towards the panchayat system? Do they value the panchayats as institutions? If so, why? To these questions, we shall now try to provide answers.

Usefulness of the Panchayat System

In order to assess the respondents' perceptions about the usefulness of the panchayat system, the question posed to them was: Do you think that the panchayat system is useful for the people of the village? The pattern of their response across four panchayats is given in Table 3.3.

An overwhelming number of respondents viewed panchayats as 'very useful' institutions. Eighty-three per cent of all respondents found them so. In Durgapur and Kasthadanga, the proportion of such respondents was more than ninety per cent. The percentage of those who consider these institutions to be 'somewhat useful' is negligible. Less than one per cent of the respondents felt that panchayats were not at all useful.

The question about usefulness of panchayats was also posed in a different manner. The respondents were asked whether they would suffer greatly if panchayat institutions were abolished. Their answers are given in Table 3.4. In order to avoid mechanical responses, this question was asked in a different context and did not follow the earlier question.

Table 3.3
Perception About Usefulness of Panchayat Institutions

Response	Kastha-danga	Baharu	Sahapur	Durgapur	Total
Very Useful	287 (98.29)	229 (76.85)	194 (64.67)	277 (92.33)	987 (82.94)
Moderately Useful	5 (1.71)	53 (17.79)	73 (24.33)	1 (0.33)	132 (11.09)
Somewhat Useful	-	14 (4.69)	8 (2.67)	5 (1.66)	27 (2.26)
Not at all Useful	-	2 (0.67)	4 (1.33)	4 (1.33)	10 (0.84)
No Response	-	-	21 (7.00)	13 (4.33)	34 (2.85)
Total	292 (100)	298 (100)	300 (100)	300 (100)	1190 (100)

Table 3.4
Respondents' Views as to Whether They Would Suffer if Panchayat Institutions are Abolished

Views	Kastha-danga	Baharu	Sahapur	Durgapur	Total
Will Suffer	275 (94.18)	269 (90.27)	152 (50.67)	288 (96.00)	984 (82.69)
Will Suffer But Not Much	14 (4.79)	26 (8.73)	109 (36.33)	6 (2.00)	155 (13.03)
Will Not Suffer	-	2 (0.67)	9 (3.00)	3 (1.00)	14 (1.17)
No Response	3 (1.03)	1 (0.33)	30 (10.00)	3 (1.00)	37 (3.10)
Total	292	298	300	300	1190

We find a striking resemblance between Tables 3.3 and 3.4. Only one per cent of the respondents said that they would not suffer if the panchayat system is abolished. While not a single respondent in Kasthadanga expressed this view, in Sahapur they constituted three per cent. Nearly eighty-three per cent of all respondents categorically stated that would suffer in the absence of the panchayat system. This figure (Table 3.4) corresponds with the percentage figure of those for whom PRIs are very useful (Table 3.3). Thirteen per cent of the respondents reported that they would suffer, but not much. Compare this with the little over thirteen per cent respondents (Table 3.3) for whom panchayats are either 'moderately' or 'somewhat' useful.

So far as inter-panchayat variations are concerned, it appears that Sahapur respondents are comparatively less enthusiastic about panchayats, though the difference in perception is a matter of degree. After all in Sahapur also, nearly ninety per cent respondents have said that panchayats are useful and that they would suffer if these are abolished. Nevertheless, the response is most positive in Kasthadanga and Durgapur Gram Panchayats, followed by Baharu.

Kasthadanga and Durgapur panchayats are held by the CPI(M). Baharu panchayat, though held by the Congress, is surrounded by areas where SUCI has a strong presence. Even in Baharu Gram Panchayat area, there are pockets where either the CPI(M) or SUCI is strong, both being cadre-based Marxist parties. Sahapur on the other hand, has been controlled by the Congress party which unlike the leftists does not have a grassroots level organisation. It is likely that the cadre-based leftist political parties (including the non-Left Front SUCI) have been far more motivated and effective in generating interest among the people and getting them to have a stake in the panchayat system.

Achievements of Panchayats

If most people think that panchayats are useful, it would be worthwhile to know why they think so. If they are taking interest in the institution, then what are the reasons.

To get an answer, we posed three sets of questions. Firstly, what do they think about certain much-publicized achievements of the West Bengal panchayats. Secondly, whether they consider panchayats as a medium for channelising their demands to the higher levels of government. And lastly, whom do they approach when they need redressal of any problem or assistance in certain kinds of situations. Tables 3.5, 3.6 and 3.7 give the pattern of responses.

Table 3.5 gives the panchayat-wise response to the question of stated achievements of panchayat institutions. Eighty-four per cent of all respondents felt that panchayats have made people conscious of their rights. The figure was as high as ninety-eight per cent in Baharu and ninety-two per cent in Durgapur Gram Panchayats. Even in Sahapur, nearly two-thirds of the respondents gave credit to panchayats for making people conscious of their rights.

For around eighty-eight per cent of the respondents, panchayats have broken the domination of landowners, *mahajans* (moneylenders) and high caste *babus* (elites). On this issue the response was fairly uniform in all the areas. In Sahapur ninety per cent of the respondents held such an opinion, while the percentage was not less than eighty-six per cent (Baharu) in any of the Gram Panchayat areas.

A large majority of the respondents (seventy-two per cent) believed that panchayats have improved the condition of the poor. In Sahapur, fifty per cent of the respondents held such a view, while over eighty per cent of the respondents subscribed to this view in Baharu and Durgapur.

An overwhelming majority (ninety-six per cent) of respondents in Durgapur felt that panchayats have provided landless people with a homestead or agricultural land. In the remaining areas, not less than three-fourths of the respondents had a similar opinion.

The respondents, however, were not as positive with respect to two other aspects of land reforms. Did panchayats ensure security of tenure to the bargadars? Fifty-nine per cent have answered in the affirmative. This is an average figure. In Kasthadanga, Baharu and Sahapur, the percentage of respondents giving an affirmative reply is less than fifty or just fifty per cent. It is only in Durgapur that as many as eighty-seven per cent believe that the lot of bargadars has improved because of the panchayat. As regards ensuring adequate wages

Table 3.5

Response to the Queries on Certain Achievements of Panchayat Institutions

Achievements	Kasthadanga			Baharu			Sahapur			Durgapur			Total		
	Yes	No	No res.	Yes	No	No res.	Yes	No	No res.	Yes	No	No res.	Yes	No.	No res.
Have made the common people conscious of their rights	239 (81.84)	26 (8.90)	27 (9.24)	291 97.65)	7 (2.34)	0	194 (64.66)	34 (11.33)	72 (24.0)	275 (91.66)	22 (7.33)	3 (1.00)	999 (83.94)	89 (7.47)	100 (8.40)
Have broken the domination of landowners, mahajans, high-caste babus	256 (87.67)	18 (6.16)	18 (6.16)	256 (85.90)	42 (14.09)	0	271 (90.33)	4 (1.33)	25 (8.33)	269 (89.66)	28 (9.33)	3 (1.00)	1052 (88.40)	92 (7.73)	46 (3.86)
Improved the condition of the poor	190 (65.06)	91 (31.16)	11 (3.76)	246 (82.55)	52 (17.44)	0	151 (50.33)	89 (29.66)	60 (20.0)	266 (88.66)	34 (11.33)	0	853 (71.68)	266 (22.35)	711 (59.74)
Ensured security of tenure of of bargadars	126 (43.15)	18 (6.16)	148 (50.68)	174 (58.38)	67 (22.48)	57 (19.12)	142 (47.33)	3 (1.00)	155 (51.66)	262 (87.33)	30 (10.00)	8 (2.66)	704 (59.15)	118 (9.91)	368 (30.92)

Contd...

Table 3.5 Contd..

Achievements	Kasthadanga			Baharu			Sahapur			Durgapur			Total		
	Yes	No	No res.	Yes	No	No res.	Yes	No	No res.	Yes	No	No res.	Yes	No.	No res.
Provided land-less people with homestead or agricultural land	252 (86.30)	16 (5.47)	24 (8.21)	225 (75.50)	69 (23.15)	4 (1.34)	226 (75.33)	16 (5.33)	58 (19.33)	289 (96.33)	11 (3.66)	0	992 (83.36)	112 (9.41)	86 (7.22)
Ensured adequate wage for agri. labour	226 (77.39)	54 (18.49)	12 (4.10)	175 (58.72)	120 (40.26)	3 (1.00)	167 (55.66)	5 (1.66)	128 (42.66)	288 (96.00)	12 (4.00)	0	856 (71.93)	191 (16.05)	143 (12.01)
Improved infra-structure such as roads, tubewells, schools etc.	240 (82.19)	48 (16.43)	4 (1.36)	287 (96.30)	10 (3.35)	1 (0.33)	193 (64.33)	78 (26.00)	29 (9.66)	276 (92.00)	21 (7.00)	3 (1.00)	996 (83.69)	157 (13.19)	37 (3.10)

Table 3.6
Response to the Proposition That Needs and Problems of Villagers Are Made Known to the State Government Through Panchayats

Response	Kasthadanga	Baharu	Sahapur	Durgapur	Total
Agree	98 (33.56)	203 (68.12)	157 (52.33)	215 (71.66)	673 (56.55)
Partially Agree	29 (9.93)	24 (8.05)	63 (21.00)	10 (3.33)	126 (10.58)
Disagree	69 (23.63)	4 (1.34)	2 (0.66)	17 (5.66)	92 (7.73)
Not Known	94 (32.19)	64 (21.47)	73 (24.33)	47 (15.66)	278 (23.36)
No Response	2 (0.68)	3 (1.00)	5 (1.66)	11 (3.66)	21 (1.76)
Total	292	298	300	300	490

Table 3.7
Agency Approached for Redressal or Assistance

Issue	Area	Agency					
		Govt. Officer	Party Leader	Panchayat Functionary	Others	No Response	Total
A hand pump is necessary for the people of the locality	Kasthadanga	3 (1.02)	7 (2.39)	272 (93.15)	3 (1.02)	7 (2.39)	292
	Baharu	-	-	298 (100.00)	-	-	298
	Sahapur	2 (0.66)	19 (6.33)	261 (87.00)	-	18 (6.00)	300
	Durgapur	1 (0.33)	27 (9.0)	262 (87.33)	-	10 (3.33)	300
	Total	6 (0.50)	53 (4.45)	1093 (91.84)	3 (0.25)	35 (2.94)	1190
Need assistance under IRDP or JRY	Kasthadanga	11 (3.76)	12 (4.10)	240 (82.19)	5 (1.71)	24 (8.21)	292
	Baharu	5 (1.67)	1 (0.33)	282 (94.63)	7 (2.34)	3 (1.00)	298
	Sahapur	-	13 (4.33)	265 (88.33)	-	22 (7.33)	300
	Durgapur	1.33 (0.33)	26 (8.66)	258 (86.00)	-	15 (5.00)	300
	Total	17 (1.42)	52 (4.36)	1045 (87.81)	12 (1.00)	64 (5.37)	1190
A school is to be repaired	Kasthadanga	10 (3.42)	-	233 (79.79)	13 (4.45)	36 (12.32)	292
	Baharu	34 (11.40)	15 (5.03)	203 (68.12)	40 (13.42)	6 (2.01)	268
	Sahapur	-	11 (3.66)	263 (87.66)	-	26 (8.66)	300
	Durgapur	2 (0.66)	27 (9.00)	261 (87.00)	-	10 (3.33)	300
	Total	46 (3.86)	53 (4.45)	960 (80.67)	53 (4.45)	78 (6.55)	1190

Contd...

Table 3.7 Contd...

Issue	Area	Agency					
		Govt. Officer	Party Leader	Panchayat Functionary	Others	No Response	Total
A road is to be built or improved	Kasthadanga	9 (3.08)	-	256 (87.67)	6 (2.05)	21 (7.19)	292
	Baharu	1 (0.33)	10 (3.35)	280 93.95)	2 (0.67)	5 (1.67)	298
	Sahapur	-	12 (4.00)	262 (87.33)	-	26 (8.66)	300
	Durgapur	2 (0.66)	27 (9.00)	260 (86.66)	-	11 (3.66)	300
	Total	12 (1.00)	49 (94.11)	1058 (88.90)	8 ((0.67)	63 (5.29)	1190
To settle village disputes	Kasthadanga	-	1 (0.34)	233 (79.79)	54 (18.49)	4 (1.36)	292
	Baharu	1 (0.33)	23 (7.71)	269 (90.26)	2 (0.67)	3 (1.00)	298
	Sahapur	1 (0.33)	13 (4.33)	262 (87.33)	-	24 (8.00)	300
	Durgapur	1 (0.33)	30 (10.00)	257 (85.66)	-	12 (4.00)	300
	Total	3 (0.25)	67 (5.63)	1021 (85.79)	56 (4.70)	43 (3.61)	1190
A situation has arisen that threaten peace in the locality	Kasthadanga	21 (7.19)	4 (1.36)	222 (76.02)	30 (10.27)	15 (5.13)	292
	Baharu	12 (4.02)	28 (9.39)	227 (76.17)	31 (10.40)	-	298
	Sahapur	-	17 (5.66)	254 (84.66)	-	29 (9.66)	300
	Durgapur	2 (0.66)	29 (9.66)	255 (85.00)		14 (4.66)	300
	Total	35 (2.94)	78 (6.55)	958 (80.50)	61 (5.12)	58 (4.87)	1190

for agricultural labour, about seventy-two per cent have given a positive reply. In Baharu and Sahapur a little less than sixty per cent of the people believe that the panchayats have ensured adequate wages for agricultural labour. So around forty per cent believe that not much has been done with respect to ensuring adequate wages for agricultural labour.

Despite this, one has to admit from the pattern of answers that majority of the rural people of West Bengal believe that substantial work has been done in the field of land reforms through the panchayats. It is true that the panchayats had been considerably involved in the land reform measures of the Left Front government especially in 'Operation Barga' and in distribution of vested land to the landless labourers. It is also true that the roles of the bureaucracy and the ruling party's front organisation, *Krishak Sabha*, were equally crucial in implementation of land reform policies of the state. But what actually established panchayats' credibility in the eyes of the people was its elected members' role in such activities as registration of bargadars, distribution of vested land, settling wage disputes between the landowner and the labourer etc. This explains why the panchayats are rated highly by the respondents in respect of achievements in certain aspects of the state's land reform measures.

The variation in the respondents' perception with regard to the achievements of panchayats need to be taken note of. In Sahapur panchayat which is controlled by Congress, the people's response to the achievements of panchayats is not as positive as of that in areas where panchayats are dominated by the CPI(M). Such variation in the respondents' perception should not only be explained by the unevenness in the performance of panchayats, but also by the role the local units of Left political parties, particularly the CPI(M), and their front organisations play, in monitoring and guiding the panchayats under their control as well as in mobilizing public opinion in favour of the panchayat institution. On the other hand, the local organisations of Congress in rural areas have, particularly since the late 1960s, been in shambles and the party's track record in supporting the panchayat movement has not been encouraging.

A large majority of respondents (eighty-four per cent) believe that panchayats have been successful in improving infrastructure like roads, tubewells etc. While the respondents of three Gram Panchayats are emphatic about this (eighty-two per cent in one area and more than ninety per cent in the other two areas) only sixty-four per cent of the people of Sahapur endorsed this achievement of the panchayat system.

Despite variations in the perceptions of respondents from different areas, the overall picture that emerges from Table 3.5, is that a large majority of people in rural West Bengal believe that panchayats have concrete achievements to their credit, especially relating to the economic improvement of the poor and land reforms.

On the other hand, for the common people of rural West Bengal, perhaps the government at the state level does not have much relevance. That is the impression one gets from Table 3.6 which seeks to explore the fact whether people view panchayats as a suitable medium for channeling their problems or demands to the state government. Not more than fifty-seven per cent of all respondents considered panchayats to be a good medium for channeling their demands to the state government, and another eleven per cent partially agreed with this view. At least one-fourth of the respondents either did not know whether panchayats performed this role or could not respond to this query.

In Sahapur and Baharu, only about one per cent of the respondents disagreed with the view that panchayats served as channels for communicating problems and demands of villages to the higher authorities.

Have panchayats become such important institutions for village people that they need not depend upon the state government or its officials for meeting their day-to-day needs? Though this question needs deeper investigation, the respondents' preferences among various agencies for redressal of, or assistance for, various problems, as reflected in Table 3.7, gives a fair indication that this, in fact, is how people think.

Respondents were asked to name the agency they would approach for assistance towards meeting six typical needs they share in common. With respect to each of these needs or issues, an overwhelming majority of respondents in each of the selected areas reported that they would approach a panchayat functionary–when a hand-pump needs to be installed, a road has to be built or repaired, a school needs repair, or assistance under JRY or IRDP is required. One should note that with regard to distribution of state largesse, government officials and political leaders (such as MLAs or influential politicians) are not viewed as very significant.

Even when it comes to the settlement of village disputes, around eighty-six per cent of the respondents said they would approach panchayats. And in a situation which has the potential of threatening peace in the locality, more than eighty per cent of the respondents said that they would prefer to go to the panchayat functionary rather than the police or magistracy.

People and Malfunctioning of Panchayats

In the absence of any statutory provision for the right to recall their elected representatives, what do people do if they are dissatisfied with the functioning of panchayats? The area-wise choice of respondents from among various agencies and options is given in Table 3.8.

On an average thirty-nine per cent of the respondents said that they would express their dissatisfaction to the concerned panchayat functionary. Despite the area-wise variation, no less than thirty-six per cent Sahapur respondents gave this answer, while at Durgapur the proportion of such respondents was forty-five per cent. It is interesting to note that as many as nearly forty per cent of the people can confront an erring panchayat representative directly to tell him that what he is doing is wrong. This is too good to believe.

A little less than one-third of the respondents (thirty per cent) said they would wait for the next election to reject the non-performing functionaries by not voting for them; nine per cent reported that they would go to the local party leader. The percentage of such respondents was twice as high (eighteen per cent) in Durgapur, revealing the controlling power the party retains over the member of an elected body.

Table 3.8
Agencies to be Approached by Respondents to Express Dissatisfaction with the Functioning of the Panchayat

Agency/forum to be approached	Kastha-danga	Baharu	Sahapur	Durgapur	Total
Panchayat Functionary	110 (37.67)	111 (37.24)	107 (35.66)	136 (45.33)	464 (38.99)
Local Party Leader	20 (6.84)	19 (6.37)	15 (5.00	55 (18.33)	109 (9.15)
Government Officials	40 (13.69)	3 (1.00)	9 (3.00)	20 (6.66)	72 (6.05)
Yearly/Half Yearly Gram Sabha Meeting	33 ((11.30)	50 (16.77)	7 (2.33)	11 (3.66)	101 (8.48)
Cast Rejecting Vote	63 (21.57)	114 (38.25)	100 (33.33)	69 (23.00)	346 (29.07)
No Response	26 ((8.90)	1 (0.33)	62 (20.66)	9 (3.00)	98 (8.23)
Total	292	298	300	300	1190

The West Bengal Panchayat Act has given powers to officials (such as the BDO, SDO, District Panchayat Officer, District Magistrate and Director of Panchayats) to take corrective actions against malfunctioning of panchayat bodies. Yet, only six per cent of the respondents felt they would approach officials in case they had problems with panchayat functionaries. Even the local party leader is seen as more effective perhaps, because, he can control his party representatives in the panchayat body. Whatever may be the reasons, it appears that the government officials are not exercising or they are being prevented from exercising their statutory powers. Had they done so, they would have been more visible to the people.

Besides, only a little more than eight per cent of the respondents consider yearly/half-yearly meetings of *Gram*

Sabha (assembly of all adults of the village(s) who are eligible to vote in the Gram Panchayat election) as the appropriate forum for voicing their dissatisfaction with regard to functioning of panchayats. In CPI(M)-held Durgapur, such respondents constituted only four per cent, while in Congress-dominated Sahapur the proportion was as low as two per cent. It is clear that, this democratic means – periodic meetings of the Gram Sabha – to correct erring panchayat functionaries is not being used by the people anywhere in rural West Bengal.

Ideally, the village assembly meetings should have been the most favoured forum to deal with this kind of problem. However, from our survey findings it appears that the role and function of this body is yet to be fully established. It would not be out of context to mention here, that in informal discussions with several people, including the office-bearers and elected functionaries of panchayats, many did not give much importance to convening the periodic meetings of the Gram Sabha, notwithstanding the clear guidelines laid down in the state Panchayat Act. Even when it is convened, the meeting is not taken seriously. Nor has there been any clear demand from the public at large for either holding of regular meetings or making them more effective.

Thus for a majority of respondents (sixty-eight per cent) there are two options: either to wait for the next election or to register their protest with the panchayat functionaries themselves. The first option leaves a panchayat representative free from accountability for five years after he is elected. The second option will hardly have any impact unless it is a forceful criticism of the action of a panchayat functionary. An ordinary person in a rural area resorting to such practice is a distant possibility. What he can do at best is to make a polite appeal to a person in authority for reconsideration of his decision. Hence the respondents' views about registering protest to the panchayat functionaries themselves have to be interpreted as making an appeal before the panchayat functionaries. Then neither of the two options noted above are effective to ensure accountability of the panchayat representatives. The most important instrument of the Gram Sabha is not at all used. In the circumstances, government officials or party leaders could be approached for correcting erring representatives.

Very few people go to the party, fewer to government officials. The result is that the panchayat representatives remain practically unaccountable to the people in the intervening period between two elections.

Panchayats Held by Opposition Parties

It is often apprehended that Gram Panchayats contr ed by opposition parties, perhaps, do not get justice from the state administration or higher level panchayats, if the latter are controlled by the ruling party (see Table 3.9). On an average, thirteen per cent respondents subscribed to this viewpoint, with panchayat-wise variation ranging from nineteen per cent (highest) at Baharu, to six percent (lowest) at Kasthadanga. If the people 'partially' agreeing to this view are also included, the percentage for all respondents goes up to twenty-three. Respondents disagreeing with the assertion constitute little less than one-fifth, Sahapur returning the lowest (eight per cent) and Kasthadanga thé highest (thirty-four per cent).

Table 3.9
Response to the View that Panchayats Held by Opposition Parties Do Not Get Justice

Response	Kastha-danga	Baharu	Sahapur	Durgapur	Total
Agree	17 (5.82)	57 (19.12)	54 (18.0)	24 (8.0)	152 (12.77)
Partially	31 (10.61)	34 (11.40)	59 (19.66)	6 (2.00)	130 (10.92)
Disagree	99 (33.90)	76 (25.50)	24 (8.0)	29 (9.66)	228 (19.15)
Cannot Say	143 (48.97)	131 (43.95)	160 (53.33)	241 (80.33)	675 (56.72)
No Response	2 (0.68)	-	3 (1.0)	-	5 (0.42)
Total	292	298	300	300	1190

However, a majority of respondents, it appears, do not have a definite view on the subject as fifty-seven per cent could not say anything with regard to this. In Durgapur, the percentage of such respondents is as high as eighty. This Gram Panchayat having always been held by the CPI(M), people here have had no experience of being under a non-ruling party regime. Even in Sahapur which is held by the opposition party, a majority of the respondents (fifty-three per cent) said that they could not say whether opposition-held Gram Panchayats were worse off. This means that most of the people, even if living under an opposition party regime, do not perceive that justice is being denied to them.

Impediments Before Panchayats

What are the factors that stand in the way of better functioning of panchayats? Six factors were identified and the respondents were asked to comment on each of them. The result is presented in Table 3.10.

Among the six factors cited as impediments to better functioning of panchayats, two are related to the devolution of power, two relate to the power structure of panchayats and the remaining two are about the quality of elected representatives of the Gram Panchayats.

Devolution of Power

There is wide divergence of opinion about this aspect across Gram Panchayats. A majority (fifty-seven per cent) of all respondents fully or partially accept that lack of sufficient funds and administrative powers is a significant impediment in the smooth functioning of panchayats. In the CPI(M)-dominated Gram Panchayats of Kasthadanga and Durgapur, about eighty and ninety per cent of the respondents, respectively, considered the insufficient devolution of power – financial and administrative – to be an important factor. In Sahapur, only four per cent respondents felt that panchayats did not have adequate administrative powers, while twelve per cent considered lack of sufficient funds as an impediment. A little less than eighty per cent of Sahapur respondents disagreed that panchayats did not

Table 3.10
Impediments before Panchayats

		Agree		Partly Agree		Disagree		No Response		Total
Panchayats	Kasthadanga	202	(69.17)	30	(10.27)	43	(14.72)	17	(5.82)	292
do not have	Baharu	61	(20.46)	69	(23.15)	168	(56.37)	-		298
enough funds	Sahapur	11	(3.66)	27	(9.0)	169	(56.33)	93	(31.0)	300
	Durgapur	245	(81.66)	30	(10.0)	25	(8.33)	-		300
	Total	519	(43.61)	156	(13.10)	405	(34.03)	110	(9.24)	1190
Panchayats	Kasthadanga	230	(78.76)	18	(6.16)	23	(7.87)	21	(7.19)	292
do not have	Baharu	19	(6.37)	46	(15.43)	233	(78.18)	-		298
enough admn.	Sahapur	1	(0.33)	13	(4.33)	207	(69.0)	79	(26.33)	300
power	Durgapur	239	(79.66)	28	(9.33)	33	(11.0)	-		300
	Total	489	(41.09)	105	(8.82)	496	(41.68)	100	(8.40)	1190
Common people are	Kasthadanga	118	(40.41)	35	(11.98)	125	(42.80)	14	(4.79)	292
not involved in	Baharu	63	(21.14)	198	(66.44)	35	(11.74)	2	(0.67)	298
decision-making	Sahapur	91	(30.33)	98	(32.66)	47	(15.66)	64	(21.33)	300
	Durgapur	52	(17.33)	35	(11.66)	193	(64.33)	20	(6.66)	300
	Total	324	(27.22)	366	(30.75)	400	(33.61)	100	(8.40)	1190
Rich and	Kasthadanga	66	(22.60)	18	(6.16)	199	(68.15)	9	(3.08)	292
influential	Baharu	157	52.68)	91	(30.53)	43	(14.42)	7	(2.34)	298
people have	Sahapur	21	(7.0)	83	(27.66)	106	(35.33)	90	(30.0)	300
a hold over	Durgapur	10	(3.33)	24	(8.0)	262	(87.33)	4	(1.33)	300
the panchayats										
	Total	254	(21.34)	216	(18.15)	610	(51.26)	110	(9.24)	1190

Contd...

Table 3.10 Contd...

		Agree		Partly agree		Disagree		No response		Total
Once elected panchayat functionaries not take interest in the well-being of the people	Kasthadanga	153	(52.39)	43	(14.72)	93	(31.84)	3	(1.02)	292
	Baharu	224	(75.16)	50	(16.77)	21	(7.04)	3	(1.00)	298
	Sahapur	176	(58.66)	68	(22.66)	7	(2.33)	49	(16.33)	300
	Durgapur	18	(6.0)	26	(8.66)	255	(85.0)	1	(0.33)	300
	Total	571	(47.98)	187	(15.71)	376	(31.59)	56	(4.70)	1190
There are dearth of suitable candidates to take charge of panchayats	Kasthadanga	104	(35.61)	50	(17.12)	121	(41.43)	17	(5.82)	292
	Baharu	127	(42.61)	121	(40.60)	44	(14.76)	6	(2.01)	298
	Sahapur	97	(32.33)	97	(32.33)	26	(8.66)	80	(26.66)	300
	Durgapur	39	(13.0)	45	(15.0)	204	(68.0)	12	(4.0)	300
	Total	367	(30.84)	313	(26.30)	395	(33.19)	115	(9.66)	1190

have sufficient administrative powers. In Baharu, more than half of the respondents (fifty-six per cent) believe that panchayats do not have enough funds whereas seventy-eight per cent disagree that the panchayats do not have enough administrative powers.

Power Structure

Respondents were asked to respond to two propositions: (i) common people are not involved in decision-making, (ii) rich and influential people have a hold over the panchayats.

A majority of respondents (fifty-eight per cent) fully or partially agreed that common people are not involved in decision-making. In Baharu as high as eighty per cent respondents held this view, while in Durgapur only around twenty-nine per cent fully or partially accepted this proposition. In Kasthadanga and Sahapur also more than fifty per cent people believed that common people do not have much role in the decision-making of panchayat activities.

On the other hand, except for Baharu, a comparatively low percentage of respondents (varying between eleven per cent and thirty-four per cent) agreed to the proposition that rich and influential people have a hold over panchayats. In Baharu more than three-fourths (eighty-three per cent) of the respondents were emphatic on this point.

Quality of Elected Representatives

Nearly two-thirds of all respondents agreed in varying degrees that once elected, the panchayat functionaries did not take much interest in the well-being of the voters. In Baharu Gram Panchayat, an overwhelming ninety-two per cent respondents held this view, while in Durgapur only fifteen per cent respondents felt so about the panchayat functionaries.

To the proposition that there is a dearth of suitable candidates who can get elected to Gram Panchayats, one-third of all respondents replied in the negative, while a majority (fifty-seven per cent) fully or partially accepted such a view. The highest proportion of such respondents was from Baharu (eighty-four per cent), while in Durgapur such respondents constituted only twenty-eight per cent.

From the responses we notice that the people of three out of four study areas agree that: (a) common people are not involved in decision-making (b) once elected, the panchayat leaders do not take interest in the well-being of the people and (c) there are dearth of suitable candidates. On the question of the power of the rich and the influential people in moulding panchayats' decisions in their favour, three Gram Panchayats disagreed, confirming their views expressed in Table 3.10. We may conclude that even though the panchayats are not controlled by the rural elite, there exists a gap between such institutions and the people, leading to lack of people's participation in panchayat functions. The gap seems to be most prominent in Sahapur where large number of respondents (sixteen to thirty-one per cent) abstained from revealing their minds on all the issues.

If we consider inter-Gram Panchayat variations, we find that the survey results of Durgapur Gram Panchayat are in contrast to the other three panchayats. According to the respondents of Durgapur, everything seems to work well as far as the power structure of the panchayat and the role of elected representatives are concerned. The overall functioning of the panchayat and its elected representatives appears to be satisfactory. An overwhelming percentage of Durgapur respondents were of the view that what actually mars or limits better functioning of the panchayats are external factors, alone, like paucity of funds (eighty-two per cent) and lack of adequate administrative powers (eighty per cent).

Even though, the large majority of Kasthadanga respondents (about eighty per cent) also see the lack of devolution of powers to be an impeding factor, more than fifty per cent agreed that the common people in the villages are not involved in decision-making; over two-thirds felt that elected functionaries hardly take interest in the welfare of the people, once voted in, and a majority of them said that there is a dearth of suitable candidates.

In Baharu and Sahapur Gram Panchayats, opinion is diametrically opposite to that of Durgapur on all counts. The majority of respondents in these two panchayats did not lay any stress on external factors like paucity of funds or lack of administrative powers. According to them, panchayats have enough financial and administrative powers, but are constrained by social and political factors.

Comparing the views of respondents from the four areas, those of Durgapur seem somewhat puzzling. Particularly, their views about involvement of common people in decision-making are not convincing, for, as we shall find later, answers to a similar question asked in a different context are contradictory. If we extricate their views on participation, then we shall find consistency in their answers both in respect of Table 3.10 as well as issues raised elsewhere. Whenever questions have been asked on the functioning of panchayats or attitude of panchayat leaders, they have consistently maintained that everything is in order. In that respect, their response as we have seen is different not only from the opposition-led panchayats of Baharu and Sahapur, but also from the CPI(M) led Kasthadanga. It is only on the question of participation that we find some inconsistency in their answers. We shall try to explain this phenomenon later.

Chapter IV

Awareness and Participation

We had hypothesized that if people value panchayat institutions – the data presented in chapter three suggests that they do – then they should know at what intervals panchayat elections are held. They should also have known that the election was due in 1993 and they should have felt dissatisfied if the state government had failed to hold the election on time. Such knowledge and consciousness of the people are the most important safeguards of democracy. Where did our respondents stand with respect to these aspects. The findings are presented in Tables 4.1, 4.2 and 4.3.

Table 4.1
Respondents' Knowledge About Interval of Panchayat Election

Response	Kastha-danga	Baharu	Sahapur	Durgapur	Total
Know	218 (74.65)	275 (92.28)	227 (75.66)	207 (69.0)	927 (77.89)
Don't Know	74 (25.34)	23 (7.71)	68 (22.66)	93 (31.0)	258 (21.68)
No Response	-	-	5 (1.66)	-	5 (0.42)
Total	292 (100)	298 (100)	300 (100)	300 (100)	1190 (100)

In response to the question on the knowledge about periodicity of panchayat elections, on an average seventy-seven per cent respondents claimed they knew about this (Table 4.1). The respondents of Baharu took the lead where the proportion of such respondents was ninety-two per cent. But the percentage of those who pleaded ignorance was highest at Durgapur (thirty-one per cent) followed by Kasthadanga (twenty-five per cent).

Table 4.2
Respondents' Knowledge About the 1993 Election

Response	Kastha-danga	Baharu	Sahapur	Durgapur	Total
Knew	131 (44.86)	238 (79.86)	265 (88.33)	245 (81.66)	879 (73.86)
Vague Idea	47 (16.09)	42 (14.09)	30 (10.00)	4 (1.33)	123 (10.33)
Not Known	114 (39.04)	18 (6.04)	-	51 (17.00)	183 (15.37)
No Response	-	-	5 (1.66)	-	5 (0.42)
Total	292 (100)	298 (100)	300 (100)	300 (100)	1190 (100)

Table 4.3
Respondents' Reaction in the Event of the 1993 Election Not Being Announced

Response	Kastha-danga	Baharu	Sahapur	Durgapur	Total
Dissatisfied	101 (56.74)	240 (85.71)	235 (78.33)	153 (61.44)	729 (72.39)
It Didn't Matter Much	52 (29.21)	30 (10.71)	9 (3.00)	88 (35.34)	179 (17.77)
No Response	25 (14.04)	10 (3.57)	56 (18..67)	8 (3.21)	99 (9.83)
Total	178 (100)	280 (100)	300 (100)	249 (100)	1007 (100)

When we come to the question of awareness about the 1993 election, we find that more than eighty per cent of respondents of Durgapur and Baharu knew that elections were due in 1993 (Table 4.2), while at Sahapur, as many as eighty-eight per cent of the respondents were aware about the 1993 elections. In contrast to the other panchayats, thirty-nine per cent of the respondents of Kasthadanga did not know as to when the panchayat elections were due and another sixteen per cent had only a vague idea about it.

How would the people have felt if the elections were not held? The question has no relevance for those who had no idea that elections were due in 1993. Of those who knew, more than eighty-five per cent respondents of Baharu and seventy-eight per cent of Sahapur felt that they would have been dissatisfied. The percentages of respondents belonging to this category in Durgapur and Kasthadanga panchayat areas are sixty-one and fifty-seven respectively. On an average, sixty-one per cent of the respondents reported that they would have been dissatisfied if the elections due in 1993 had not been held (Table 4.3).

Despite differences in degree among respondents living in different panchayat areas, a majority of them were aware about the periodicity of panchayat elections, knowledgeable about the necessity of holding elections in 1993 and conscious that it was wrong to postpone an election which is statutorily due. This is yet another indication of the fact that people attach much value to the panchayat system and they are well aware and conscious about the holding of regular elections for maintaining the democratic character of the panchayat system. Such knowledge and consciousness of common voters, however, appears to be somewhat less in the two panchayats controlled by the ruling party. In the absence of support data, we do not want to draw any conclusion on the point, but the finding, it has to be admitted, is puzzling.

Information About the Elections and Its Sources

When did the respondents get to know about the date of the panchayat election and what were the sources of such information? Tables 4.4 and 4.5 provide the answers.

Table 4.4
Period of Prior Information About Election Date

Response	Kastha-danga	Baharu	Sahapur	Durgapur	Total
8 Weeks	69 (23.63)	63 (21.14)	121 (40.33)	65 (21.66)	318 (26.72)
6 Weeks	35 (11.980	39 (13.08)	59 (19.66)	8 (2.66)	141 (11.84)
4 Weeks	107 (36.64)	20 (6.71)	85 (28.33)	64 (21.33)	276 (23.19)
2 Weeks	52 (17.80)	1 (0.33)	24 (8.0)	56 (18.66)	133 (11.17)
1 Week	14 (4.79)	165 (55.36)	4 (1.33)	81 (27.0)	264 (22.18)
No Knowledge	15 (5.13)	10 (3.35)	-	7 (2.33)	32 (2.68)
No Response	-	-	7 (2.33)	19 (6.33)	26 (2.18)
Total	292	298	300	300	1190

The notification of the state government announcing the election date was issued on 10 March, 1993 – about eleven weeks before the date of election, 31 May, 1993. The last date for filing nomination papers of candidates was 26 April, that is five weeks before election. Those who knew about the election date six to eight weeks before must be quite enlightened, because the election campaign does not start picking up momentum till the names of the contesting candidates are finalized. The list of final candidates is not published before four weeks from the date of the election.

Table 4.5
Sources of Information About the Election Date

Source	Kastha-danga	Baharu	Sahapur	Durgapur	Total
Relatives/ Friends	31 (11.19)	10 (3.47)	149 (50.85)	39 (14.23)	229 (19.24)
Panchayat Leaders	55 (19.86)	22 (7.64)	21 (7.17)	36 (13.14)	134 (11.84)
Political Parties	43 (15.52)	119 (41.32)	30 (10.24)	53 (19.34)	245 (21.64)
Newspapers	34 (12.27)	17 (5.90)	18 (6.14)	39 (14.23)	108 (9.54)
Radio/TV	39 (14.08)	2 (0.69)	9 (3.07)	23 (8.39)	73 (6.45)
Everybody Was Talking About It	70 (25.27)	118 (40.97)	66 (22.53)	83 (30.29)	337 (29.77)
Others	5 (1.81)	-	-	1 (0.36)	6 (0.53)
Total	277 (100)	288 (100)	293 (100)	274 (100)	1132 (100)

Yet we find that thirty-nine per cent of the respondents knew about the election date six weeks before, and another twenty-three per cent knew of it four weeks prior to election. Thus sixty-two per cent of the respondents knew about the election date a month in advance. This could be regarded as encouraging. However in Durgapur, only twenty-four per cent of the respondents had this information six weeks before and another twenty-one per cent four weeks before election. As the election date advances, more and more people get involved and thus we notice that one week before the election date more than ninety-four per cent respondents knew about the event, leaving around five per cent who did not appear to be interested in the electoral process.

The respondents were also asked to reveal their sources of information. The biggest source of information appears to be people themselves (Table 4.5). The category 'everybody was talking about it' scored around thirty per cent, the highest among all categories of sources of information. If this is clubbed with the source termed 'relatives and friends', these together become the principal sources of information for over fifty per cent of the respondents. In Sahapur, however, half the respondents have identified 'relatives and friends' as their source of information. It is possible that some of them have not been able to distinguish between the categories 'relatives and friends' and 'everybody was talking about it'. The conclusion is clear: the panchayat election is a big event in the village and it is difficult for people not to take notice of it. Political parties and panchayat functionaries were the next important sources of information. A little over one-third of the respondents claimed that they came to know about the panchayat election from these sources.

The reach and the impact of mass media, such as newspapers, radio/TV, in the dissemination of information regarding election date seems to have been marginal. This is, however, not surprising given the socio-economic status of the respondents.

Sources of information about the names of the candidates and their symbols were also the same, as can be seen from Table 4.6. Here also we find that the two categories of information sources, 'relatives and friends' and 'everybody was talking about it', was referred to by nearly forty per cent of the respondents. The sources, 'political parties' and 'panchayat leaders' were cited by one-third of the respondents. Publicity activities of candidates seem to have played a small role as a source of information. Only about fifteen per cent of the respondents indicated publicity materials as a source of information about either the names of candidates or their symbols.

Tables 4.5 and 4.6 clearly demonstrate that the flow of electoral information is not controlled by the political parties alone. Even though they play a significant role in disseminating such information, people have their own sources as well and this is an indication of opening up of rural society.

Table 4.6
Source of Information About the Names of Candidates and Their Symbols

Source	Kastha-danga	Baharu	Sahapur	Durgapur	Total
Relatives and Friends	20 (6.84)	6 (2.01)	134 (44.66)	25 (8.33)	185 (15.54)
Panchayat Leaders	27 (9.24)	26 (8.72)	11 (3.66)	17 (5.66)	81 (6.80)
Political Parties	67 (22.94)	100 (33.55)	48 (16.0)	102 (34.00)	317 (26.63)
Poster/ Handbills	12 (4.10)	8 (2.68)	18 (6.0)	5 (1.66)	43 (3.61)
Wall Writing/ Public Announce-ment, Meeting etc.	63 (21.57)	24 (8.05)	11 (3.66)	34 (11.33)	132 (11.09)
'Everybody Was Talking About It'	73 (25.0)	128 (42.95)	19 (6.33)	64 (21.33)	284 (23.86)
Candidates	20 (6.84)	-	-	16 (5.33)	36 (3.02)
Others	3 (1.02)	-	-	-	3 (0.25)
No Response	7 (2.39)	6 (2.01)	59 (19.66)	37 (12.33)	109 (9.15)
Total	292	298	300	300	1190

The Election Campaign and the People

What is the extent and nature of the election campaign in a panchayat election and what kind of interest do people take in it? Tables 4.7 and 4.8 highlight these aspects.

Table 4.7
Area-wise Exposure to Election Campaign

Activity	Area	More Than Once		Once		Never		No Response		Total
Approached by the candidates or their supporters	Kasthadanga	257	(88.01)	20	(6.84)	13	(4.45)	2	(0.68)	292
	Baharu	204	(68.45)	2	(0.67)	92	(30.87)	-		228
	Sahapur	69	(23.0)	5	(1.66)	217	(72.33)	9	(3.0)	300
	Durgapur	11	(3.66)	169	(56.33)	120	(40.00)	-		300
	Total	541	(45.46)	196	(16.48)	442	(37.14)	11	(0.92)	1190
Witnessed processions organized in favour of the candidates	Kasthadanga	259	(88.69)	23	(7.87)	10	(3.42)	-		292
	Baharu	288	(96.64)	1	(0.33)	9	(3.02)	-		298
	Sahapur	99	(33.0)	8	(2.06)	185	(61.66)	8	(2.66)	300
	Durgapur	9	(3.0)	69	(23.0)	222	(74.0)	-		300
	Total	655	(55.04)	101	(8.48)	426	(35.73)	8	(0.67)	1190
Received hand bills issued by the candidates or political parties	Kasthadanga	254	(86.98)	38	(13.01)	-		-		292
	Baharu	277	(92.95)	15	(5.03)	6	(2.01)	-		298
	Sahapur	278	(92.66)	12	(4.0)	-		10	(3.33)	300
	Durgapur	230	(76.66)	49	(16.33)	21	(7.0)	-		300
	Total	1039	(87.31)	114	(9.57)	27	(2.26)	10	(0.84)	1190

Table 4.8
Respondents' Observation of Visual Display in the Election Campaign

Response	Kastha-danga	Baharu	Sahapur	Durgapur	Total
Seen	287 (98.28)	275 (92.28)	277 (92.33)	268 (89.33)	1107 (93.02)
Not Seen	3 (1.02)	13 (4.36)	4 (1.33)	13 (4.33)	33 (2.77)
No Response	2 (.68)	10 (3.35)	19 (6.33)	19 (6.33)	50 (4.20)
Total	292	298	300	300	1190

Table 4.7 shows that a little less than two-thirds (sixty-two per cent) of the respondents across the four panchayats have been approached by the candidates at least once or more than once. On an average, about forty per cent of the respondents remained untouched, but the position in Sahapur is much worse than the average, where, as many as seventy-two per cent of the respondents said that they had never been approached by candidates or their supporters.

Nearly two-thirds of the respondents have witnessed processions organized in favour of candidates either once or more than once. However, here again, sixty-two per cent of the respondents of Sahapur and nearly three-fourths of the respondents of Durgapur have never seen such processions. From our findings it appears that whether it was the opposition party-led Sahapur or the CPI(M) stronghold of Durgapur, the response of the people was the same.

More than ninety per cent respondents received handbills issued by the candidates or parties and an almost similar number of respondents noticed slogans, symbols and names of candidates painted on walls, hoardings etc (Table 4.8). There was not much area-wise variation regarding this aspect.

We may conclude that even though there were exceptions, the election campaign was conducted on a large scale. During our field visits as well, we witnessed active campaigning and noted that people's attendance in public meetings at some places was very high. The intensity of campaigning, however, seemed less where the area was under the absolute control of one party, as in Durgapur. Here all the seats of the Gram Panchayat were won by the CPI(M) in 1988 and, subsequently, in 1993. The areas surrounding the Gram Panchayat are also fully under the control of the party, and the other parties are practically non-existent. That may explain why the extent of campaigning was less in Durgapur compared to other areas. Lack of intensity of campaigning in Sahapur, on the other hand, can be explained by the organizational weakness of the political parties at the local level.

Campaigning is one side of the story. How did the people react to the campaigning? The answer to this is presented in Tables 4.9, 4.10 and 4.11.

West Bengal was the first state in the country to give shape to what has come to be known as 'political panchayats, that is to say, panchayats where elections are contested by political parties, like elections to Parliament or state assemblies. Again, it is in West Bengal that the Left parties led by the CPI(M) and their front organizations have been very active, with their organizational structures extending down to the grassroots level. It is, therefore, widely believed that in West Bengal the political parties and their front organizations are making a major contribution to the process of political mobilization. If this is true, then it should be a case of the people being keenly interested in the election campaign. Our findings given in Tables 4.9, 4.10 and 4.11, however, provide a different picture.

On an average, only twenty-four per cent of the respondents were found to have taken keen interest in the election campaign (Table 4.9). The extent of active interest varied from a mere seven per cent of the respondents in Baharu to one-third respondents in Sahapur, where another thirty-six per cent claimed to have shown moderate interest in the election campaign. On the other hand, those who said that they had no interest at all in the election campaign, constituted a little less than half (forty-seven per cent) of the respondents in Kasthadanga, followed by thirty-five per cent in Durgapur. Ironically, both areas are under the influence of the CPI(M).

Table 4.9
Interest in the Election Campaign

Extent of Interest Taken	Kastha-danga	Baharu	Sahapur	Durgapur	Total
Keen	84 (28.76)	21 (7.04)	96 (32.0)	80 (26.66)	281 (23.61)
Moderate	42 (14.38)	83 (27.85)	107 (35.66)	-	232 (19.49)
Slight	29 (9.93)	136 (45.63)	65 (21.66)	110 (36.66)	340 (28.57)
Not At All	137 (46.91)	58 (19.46)	30 (10.0)	106 (35.33)	331 (27.81)
No Response	-	-	2 (0.66)	4 (1.33)	6 (0.50)
Total	292	298	300	300	1190

When we come to the findings relating to attendance in public meetings, we note that thirty per cent of all respondents said that they had attended public meetings more than once (Table 4.10). Area-wise, the proportion of such respondents varied from fifty-nine per cent (Baharu) to just three per cent (Durgapur). In the latter area, another twenty-four per cent claimed to have attended public meetings just once. In other words, in Durgapur more than seventy per cent of the respondents did not find the election meetings worth attending. The same is true of Sahapur panchayat area where seventy-two per cent of the respondents reported never having attended any meeting at all. Even the lowest figure of non-attendance among all the panchayat areas was as high as forty per cent in Baharu. This simply means that a large number of respondents did not have any interest at all in what the leaders of political parties had to say on the election issues.

Table 4.10
Attendance in Public Meetings Organised by Political Parties

Extent of Interest Taken	Kastha-danga	Baharu	Sahapur	Durgapur	Total
More Than Once	102 (34.93)	177 (59.39)	69 (23.0)	10 (3.33)	358 (30.08)
Once	19 (6.50)	3 (1.00)	6 (2.0)	73 (24.33)	101 (8.48)
Never	170 (58.21)	118 (39.59)	215 (71.66)	217 (72.33)	720 (60.50)
No Response	1 (0.34)	-	10 (3.33)	-	11 (0.92)
Total	292	298	300	300	1190

Table 4.11
Awareness of Promises of Political Parties During Election

Extent of Interest Taken	Kastha-danga	Baharu	Sahapur	Durgapur	Total
Thoroughly	91 (31.16)	18 (6.04)	54 (18.0)	19 (6.33)	182 (15.29)
To a Large Extent	71 (24.31)	81 (27.18)	119 (39.66)	-	271 (22.77)
Vaguely	70 (23.97)	76 (25.50)	81 (27.0)	141 (47.0)	368 (30.92)
Not At All	60 (20.54)	123 (41.27)	24 (8.0)	135 (45.0)	342 (28.73)
No Response	-	-	22 (7.33)	5 (1.66)	27 (2.26)
Total	292	298	300	300	1190

A similar picture emerges in respect of the respondents' awareness of promises made by the political parties/candidates. While thirty-eight per cent were aware either thoroughly or to a large extent of the political parties' promises, about sixty per cent had only a vague idea or no idea about such promises (Table 4.11). Area-wise variations were as follows: Durgapur had the highest number of respondents (ninety-two per cent) who claimed that they knew only slightly or nothing about the promises of political parties and Sahapur recorded the least percentage (thirty-five per cent) of such respondents.

This brings us to a grim reality that a large number of people belonging to the SC and ST categories, generally referred to as weaker sections of society, seem to have been left out of the politicization process or have been taken for granted. This is all the more disturbing in the case of Durgapur Gram Panchayat which lies in Burdwan district where the membership of front organizations of the CPI(M) is said to be one of the largest in the state.

In the case of Sahapur also it would not suffice to say that the organizational strength of the Congress is in disarray, and hence the extent of people's involvement in election meetings was fairly low. In fact, the very absence of any organized effort by the party which has been traditionally dominant in the area, should have prompted other political parties to seek the support of people in Sahapur through their mass contact programmes. This is the logic of the open, competitive political system which all political parties have seemingly failed to grasp.

Exposure to Media

Though the mass media can play a great role in politicization, it is well-known that in India, the impact of print and electronic media on an electoral process, in which only rural people are involved, is very little. For such media to be accessible, the level of literacy and income of the people has to be fairly high. In rural West Bengal, high levels of either education or income do not appear to have been achieved to permit large sections of the masses to be exposed to the mass media. This is confirmed by the data presented in Table 4.12.

Among the respondents, the highest percentage of newspaper readers were found at Baharu (twenty-three per cent) followed by Kasthadanga (thirteen per cent), while the corresponding figure for Sahapur and Durgapur panchayat areas was seven per cent (Table 4.12). On the other hand, those who have never read a newspaper – not even occasionally – constitute as high as seventy per cent of the respondents (highest) in Durgapur. To this may be added those who did not respond (six per cent). The corresponding percentage of respondents in this category in Baharu was also high (fifty-four per cent).

The obvious reason is illiteracy and poverty. For, if we tally the figures of those who never had occasion to read a newspaper with that of illiterates or those who had only studied upto primary level (see Chapter Two, Table 2.3), we will find that these figures almost match. There is also a definite correlation with the ownership of landed property (see Table 2.6). The higher the percentage of the poor and illiterate, the higher the percentage of people never exposed to newspaper reading.

As regards regularly listening to radio programmes or news, the findings reveal poor exposure. While at Durgapur and Sahapur, eight per cent of the respondents and less, reported listening to the radio regularly, the highest percentage of such respondents, recorded from Kasthadanga, was only twenty-eight per cent.

The situation is slightly better in the case of listening to radio, for to be a listener one does not have to be literate. Moreover, the radio is a familiar consumer product in rural areas. Even though there may not be many regular listeners, the number of those who listen to radio programmes at least occasionally is considerable. This means that people have access to either community sets or to radios belonging to others. If their number is added to those who are regular radio listeners, around sixty per cent of the respondents were found to be listening to radio programmes. In Durgapur, however, even after including such respondents the percentage is less than thirty per cent.

Table 4.12
Extent of Media Exposure

Frequency	Kasthadanga			Baharu			Sahapur			Durgapur			Total		
	News	Radio	TV	News	Radio	TV	News	Radio	TV	News	Radio	TV	News	Radio	TV
Regularly	38 (13.0)	82 (28.0)	33 (11.30)	69 (23.1)	38 (12.75)	34 (11.4)	20 (6.6)	24 (8.0)	34 (11.3)	21 (7.0)	18 (6.0)	14 (4.66)	148 (12.43)	162 (13.61)	115 (9.66)
Occasio-nally	81 (27.7)	112 (38.3)	67 (22.9)	68 (22.8)	162 (54.3)	84 (28.1)	54 (18.0)	151 (50.3)	24 (8.0)	51 (17.0)	67 (22.3)	31 (10.33)	254 (21.34)	492 (41.34)	206 (17.31)
Never	173 (59.2)	93 (31.8)	192 (65.7)	161 (54.2)	98 (32.8)	180 (60.4)	191 (63.6)	112 (37.3)	225 (75)	211 (70.3)	192 (64)	239 (79.66)	736 (61.84)	500 (42.01)	836 (70.25)
No Response						35	13 (11.6)	17 (4.3)	17 (5.66)	23 (5.66)	16 (7.66)	52 (5.33)	36 (4.36)	33 (3.02)	(2.77)

It is natural that the reach of TV should be even narrower. On an average, around ten per cent respondents reported watching TV regularly and around seventy per cent said that they did not have any access to this medium. Area-wise, the lowest percentage of such respondents – with no access – was still as high as sixty per cent in Baharu.

Voting Decision and Expectations From Candidates

A person considers several factors in deciding whom to vote for. Our respondents were asked to name one among three important factors: past performance, policies of the party to which the candidate belongs, and personal qualities of the candidate.

Thirty-seven per cent of the respondents considered the 'past performance' of the candidate/party to be the most important factor, for about one-third of them it was the 'policies of the contesting parties', while twenty-seven per cent looked for 'personal qualities' of the candidates (Table 4.13). It is interesting to note, that despite intensive activities of the political parties, especially the Left parties, in rural West Bengal, the party and its policies are not considered to be the most important factors in the voting decision of the respondents.

Table 4.13
Factors Considered Important by Respondents in Voting

Factor	Kastha-danga	Baharu	Sahapur	Durgapur	Total
Past Performance of the Candidate	53 (18.15)	195 (65.43)	80 (26.66)	110 (36.66)	438 (36.80)
Policies of the Party to Which the Candidate Belongs	111 (38.01)	71 (23.82)	75 (25.0)	127 (42.33)	384 (32.26)
Personal Qualities of the Candidate	126 (43.15)	32 (10.73)	105 (35.0)	60 (20.0)	323 (27.14)
No Response	2 (0.68)	-	40 (13.33)	3 (1.0)	45 (3.78)
	292	298	300	300	490

It is only in Durgapur, that forty-two per cent of the respondents gave this factor first preference, while for another thirty-seven per cent, the past performance of the candidate was the first criterion to be considered.

Thus, while the party is not unimportant, other factors are equally or more important. At least in two places (Kasthadanga and Sahapur), the most important factor was personal qualities of a candidate, while in another place (Baharu), as many as sixty-five per cent of the respondents considered 'past performance' as the most important factor in voting decision.

Table 4.14
The Most Important Quality Expected of a Candidate

Quality	Kastha-danga	Baharu	Sahapur	Durgapur	Total
Honesty	172 (58.90)	181 (60.73)	182 (60.66)	171 (57.0)	706 (59.32)
Sensitivity to the Sufferings of the Poor	71 (24.31)	77 (25.83)	94 (31.0)	67 (22.33)	309 (25.74)
Belongs to the Political Party One Supports	45 (15.41)	38 (12.75)	17 (5.66)	58 (19.33)	158 (13.27)
Belongs to the Same Religion/ Caste	4 (1.36)	2 (0.67)	7 (2.33)	4 (1.33)	17 (1.42)
	292	298	300	300	1190

Among the personal qualities expected of candidate, honesty seems to be the most important factor with about sixty per cent of the respondents giving it the highest score (Table 4.14). For a little over one-fourth of the respondents, sensitivity to the sufferings of the poor was the most important quality. It is interesting to note that not more than thirteen per cent regarded the party to which a candidate belongs as the only factor to be taken into account. People expect that the candidates chosen by the party should have important personal qualities, among which honesty is rated first by many. Another important point that deserves attention is the fact that, in West Bengal, contrary to what happens in many north Indian states, factors like caste or religion do not play a significant role in the voters' decisions. Our survey shows that not even two per cent of the respondents would have liked to vote on considerations of either caste or religion (Table 4.14).

Reservation of Seats

The issue of reservation of seats for women and SCs and STs in panchayats has come to the forefront after the adoption of the 73rd Constitution Amendment. Prior to that, some states had already made a similar provision in their panchayat acts. Previously in West Bengal, there was no such provision. There were, however, provisions for nomination of women as well as SC and ST members if such persons were not represented in panchayat bodies through elections. Even though in many cases the lower caste people could find representation in panchayat bodies, as in Burdwan, women were practically invisible.[1] Anticipating the constitutional amendment and also to correct the imbalance, West Bengal included the reservation provision in its 1992 amendments of the Panchayat Act.

Thus from an almost non-existent status (less than one per cent of total elected representatives), suddenly women were required to occupy 24,895 seats out of a total of 71,120 seats in all three tiers. This indeed was a very big jump. Doubts were expressed as to whether women in sufficient numbers would come forward to contest so many seats.

However, much before the 1993 elections, the Left parties, particularly the CPI(M) and its women's wing, *Ganatantrik Mahila Samiti* (GMS) and the West Bengal state unit of the All India Democratic Women's Association had organized numerous meetings at the grassroots level across the state.

Ms Shyamali Gupta, the state secretary of GMS, told us that one of the objectives of those meetings was to raise awareness on the issue of reservation for women among the public at large.[2] Such awareness-building exercises seems to have paid rich dividends. It will be seen in Chapter Eight that the seats reserved for women were keenly contested.

But what about the people in general? What is their level of awareness about and attitude towards the reservation of seats for women and the SC/STs? Is it positive or negative? To test this, we posed before respondents four questions. Their answers are provided in Tables 4.15 to 4.17.

Table 4.15
Awareness of Statutory Provision for Reservation of Seats for Women in Panchayat Bodies

	Kastha-danga	Baharu	Sahapur	Durgapur	Total
Aware	234 (80.13)	297 (99.66)	268 (89.33)	137 (45.65)	936 (78.65)
Not Aware	58 (19.86)	1 (0.33)	23 (7.65)	156 (52.0)	238 (20.0)
No Response	-	-	9 (3.0)	7 (2.33)	16 (1.34)
	292	298	300	300	1190

Table 4.16
Awareness of Statutory Provisions of Reservation of Seats for SCs/STs in Panchayat Bodies

	Kastha-danga	Baharu	Sahapur	Durgapur	Total
Aware	186 (63.69)	298 (100.0)	197 (65.66)	128 (42.66)	809 (67.98)
Not Aware	106 (36.30)	-	94 (31.33)	164 (54.66)	364 (30.58)
No Response	- -	-	9 (3.0)	8 (2.66)	17 (1.42)
	292	298	300	300	1190

It is apparent from Table 4.15 that nearly eighty per cent respondents across the four panchayat areas reported that they were aware of the provision for reservation of seats for women in panchayats. In Sahapur, an overwhelming ninety per cent of the respondents were aware, while in Baharu almost 100 per cent knew about this provision.

Curiously, once again, over half the Durgapur respondents expressed ignorance about the issue. Why did these people not know when others did need further examination. It is all the more perplexing when it is seen that more than half the Durgapur respondents (fifty-five per cent) were not even aware of the reservation of seats for SCs and STs (Table 4.16). It is necessary to remember that nearly forty-eight per cent of the respondents of this panchayat area belong to the SC/ST category (See Chapter Two, Table 2.4).

In the other three panchayat areas, the situation is different, since two-thirds and a little less than two-thirds of the respondents in Sahapur and Kasthadanga respectively were aware of the provision and in Baharu 100 percent knew about it.

In response to the question as to whether reservation for women has been a step in the right direction, seventy-one per cent and sixty-seven per cent of the respondents of Kasthadanga and Baharu respectively said, 'yes', whereas the corresponding numbers in Sahapur and Durgapur panchayat areas were much lower, being twenty-eight per cent and thirty-five per cent respectively (Table 4.17). For all respondents in the four panchayat areas taken together, fifty per cent held the view that reservation of seats for women in panchayat bodies has been a step in the right direction. Indeed the positive response was overwhelming in three panchayats, being above two-thirds in Kasthadanga and Sahapur and cent per cent in Baharu.

Interestingly, in Sahapur panchayat nearly one-fifth of the respondents were of the view that it (i.e. the reservation) would create complications, a little less than of the one-fourth respondents believed that women were 'unsuitable' and thirteen per cent had nothing to say on this issue.

In Durgapur, those who declined to give any response to this question constituted as many as fifty-four per cent of the respondents. It may be recalled that women constituted forty-two per cent of the respondents at Durgapur and twenty-seven per cent at Sahapur. In Baharu, less than one-fifth of the respondents were women (See Chapter Two, Table 2.2).

Table 4.17
Response to the Proposition that Reservation of Seats for Women and SC/ST Has Been a Step in Right Direction

Response	Kasthadanga		Baharu		Sahapur		Durgapur		Total	
	For Women	For SC/ST	For Women	For SC/ST	For Women	For SC/ST	For Women	For SC/ST	For Women	For SC/ST
Agree	208 (71.2)	195 (66.7)	196 (67.1)	228 (76.5)	85 (28.3)	144 (48)	104 (34.6)	110 (36.6)	593 (49.83)	677 (56.89)
Agree to Some Extent	20 (6.8)	5 (1.7)	15 (5.0)	5 (1.6)	47 (15.6)	42 (14.0)	2 (6.6)	-	84 (7.05)	52 (4.36)
It Was Necessary	4 (1.3)	2 (0.6)	49 (16.7)	7 (2.3)	-	1 (0.3)	-	84	53 (4.45)	10 (1.76)
It Will Create Complications	6 (2.0)	2 (0.6)	19 (6.3)	7 (2.3)	58 (19.3)	12 (4.0)	1 (0.3)	84 (7.05)		21 (1.76)
Women/ SC & ST Are Unsuitable	12 (4.1)	3 (1.0)	9 (3.0)	51 (17.1)	70 (23.3)	12 (4.0)	30 (10.0)	16 (5.3)	121 (10.16)	82 (6.89)
No Response	42 (14.3)	85 (29.0)	10 (3.4)	-	40 (13.3)	89 (29.6)	163 (54.3)	174 (58.0)	255 (21.42)	348 (29.24)
Total	292	292	298	298	300	300	300	300	300	1190

Yet, more than two-thirds of the Baharu respondents were positive about the issue compared to one-third in Durgapur.

A majority of all respondents felt that reservation of seats for SCs and STs has been a positive step (Table 4.17). In Durgapur panchayat area, only thirty-seven per cent of the respondents were of this view, while a little less than sixty per cent gave no response. Ironically, around forty-eight per cent of the respondents from this panchayat area belong to the scheduled categories for whose benefit the reservation provision was introduced. On the other hand, in Baharu where only eighteen per cent respondents belonged to the SC and ST categories, seventy-seven per cent of the respondents expressed the view that reservation of seats for these communities had been a step in the right direction.

If the findings on perceptions relating to the issue of reservation for women and those for SCs and STs are compared, we notice that supporters of reservation for SCs/STs outnumber, though not by a significant margin, those for women. The percentage of respondents, in all the areas, subscribing to the view that reservation of seats for women will create complications or that women are unsuitable, is higher than those who think in the same terms with regard to reservation of seats for SCs and STs.

This is not surprising, since in many spheres, including reservation of seats in state legislatures and Parliament, people are accustomed to the special benefits given to the SC/ST category. The application of the same principle for women in panchayat bodies is a novel experience for the electorate. Nevertheless, in Kasthadanga and Baharu, about seventy per cent of the respondents did consider it a step in the right direction.

If the four panchayat areas of our study give an approximate picture of the realities of the entire state, we can say that at least fifty per cent of the people in rural West Bengal are positive about the need for fair representation being given to both women and SC/ST candidates in panchayat bodies.

Notes and References

1. G.K. Lieten, "Caste, Gender and Class in Panchayats: Case of Bardhaman, West Bengal", *Economic and Political Weekly*, 18 July 1992.

2. Personal interview at Calcutta, 10 June 1993.

Chapter V

Participation or Alienation

One of the objectives of our study was to capture the feelings of the ordinary people about themselves as voters in the panchayat elections. Do they think that they matter in how panchayats function, or have become apathetic, because they feel they are powerless.

To assess this, we posed four questions to the respondents. Firstly, we asked them whether they would/had cast their vote in the elections.[1] Our assumption was that people would answer in the negative if they had developed a sense of apathy. Our findings indicate that an overwhelming number of respondents (ninety per cent) had, or intended to, cast their votes (Table 5.1). The area-wise variation was: eighty-one per cent at Sahapur (lowest), 100 per cent at Baharu and nearly 100 per cent at Kasthadanga.

However, a shadow falls on such an overwhelmingly positive attitude when we look at the responses to the three other questions posed. The respondents were asked to react to the following propositions: 1) 'People like me do not have any say in what panchayats do'; 2) 'It does not make much difference whether people like me vote or not'; 3) 'I cast/will cast my vote, because:

(a) Persons around me persuade/d me to vote
(b) Party leaders persuade/d me to vote
(c) I feel/felt it is/was my duty to cast my vote
(d) Panchayat functionaries cannot be made responsible to the people, unless voters take interest in casting their votes.'

The response to these questions presents a mixed picture. Roughly seventy per cent of the respondents in Kasthadanga and Baharu disagreed with the proposition that common people do not have any say in what panchayats do. While more than sixty per cent at Sahapur and fifty-three per cent at Durgapur agreed with it, one-third of the respondents in Sahapur expressed no view on this issue (Table 5.2).

Table 5.1
Response to the Question: Will You/Have You Cast Your Vote

Response	Kastha-danga	Baharu	Sahapur	Durgapur	Total
Yes	290 (99.31)	298 (100.00)	242 (80.66)	247 (82.33)	1077 (90.50)
No	2 (0.68)	-	-	6 (2.0)	8 (0.67)
No Response	-	-	58 (19.33)	47 (15.66)	105 (8.82)
Total	292	298	300	300	1190

Table 5.2
Response to the Question:
'People Like Us Do Not Have Any Say in What Panchayats Do'

Response	Kastha-danga	Baharu	Sahapur	Durgapur	Total
Agree	29 (9.93)	16 (5.36)	182 (60.66)	160 (53.33)	387 (32.52)
Partially Agree	2 (0.68)	77 (25.83)	7 (2.33)	-	86 (7.22)
Disagree	208 (71.23)	205 (68.79)	9 (3.0)	138 (46.0)	560 (47.05)
No Response	53 (18.15)	-	102 (34.0)	2 0.66)	157 (13.19)
	292	298	300	300	1190

With regard to the second question, two-thirds of all respondents disagreed with the idea that it did not matter if people like them voted or not. In Kasthadanga, such respondents were as many as ninety-five per cent of the total (Table 5.3). In contrast to the negligible number of respondents agreeing to the proposition in three panchayat areas, in Durgapur more than half the respondents felt that whether they cast their votes or not did not matter in the panchayat election. Taking Tables 5.2 and 5.3 together, we are forced to conclude that, by and large, people in Durgapur to a greater degree and those of Sahapur to a lesser degree, feel alienated from the panchayat institutions.

One may argue that if that be the case why did eighty-two per cent of the Durgapur respondents (Table 5.1) cast their votes? If they think that they do not matter in the panchayat and votes of people like them have no importance, why would so many people take the trouble of going to the polling stations and casting their votes?

For an answer, we have to look at Table 5.4. The response of Durgapur respondents seems puzzling. Had they said that they had been persuaded by persons around them or by leaders of political parties to cast their vote, that would have been understandable. But such respondents constituted only eight per cent, whereas seventy per cent respondents said that they had, or would cast their vote because they felt "it was their duty" to do so. Given the background of the respondents, the answer does not sound convincing. Did the respondents of Durgapur voice a tutored slogan without understanding its meaning?

We expected that respondents who are more mature and conscious would say that they vote because panchayat functionaries cannot be made responsible to the people, unless people take interest in casting their votes. We wanted to test whether people in rural West Bengal are aware of this cardinal principle of democracy, that people's representatives are responsible to the people.

We find that two-thirds of the Kasthadanga respondents and over half of the Baharu respondents have passed the test in stating that their chief reason for voting was to elect panchayat representatives who would be accountable to the people. Even in Sahapur, nearly half of the respondents asserted this as the main reason for voting.

The above discussion raises hope as well as doubts for the future of the panchayat system in the state. At one end, we find a conscious electorate as in Kasthadanga and Baharu. At the other, we find an electorate which is alienated to a greater or lesser degree as in Durgapur and Sahapur panchayat areas. Suspicion lingers as to the manner in which the panchayat is run in Durgapur. The people seem to be happy with their panchayat and, as we have seen earlier, according to them all is going well with what the panchayat is doing. At the same time they think that common people do not have much say in the mode of functioning of panchayat and individual votes of the common people are not of much importance. The same respondents asserted in Table 3.16 (see Chapter Three) that common people were involved in the decision-making of panchayat bodies. The apparent contradiction in answers to the questions asked in different context can be explained if we assume the existence of a relationship between the panchayat and the people similar to the one that exists between a benefactor and a beneficiary. They are all praise for what panchayats do and the manner in which these are done, but do not think that they have control over the institution. Is it then to be inferred that here is a panchayat which is benevolent and efficient, but does not give priority to further the process of popular participation? If that is the case then the findings would lend support to the view that the West Bengal panchayats have laid emphasis on management, but have failed to empower the poor. Thus, 'the people, i.e. the poor majority, cannot be said to be determining politics'[2] and even through 'the representation of the poor has been increased in the institutions of power...by and large their representation has not resulted in any significant increase in their control over their institution.'[3]

One of the prerequisites of a democratic polity is that people should independently decide whom they should choose as their representative and should not be guided by narrow family ties or caste loyalties. It is gratifying to note that respondents in all the areas expressed that they had full autonomy in respect of their decision about whom to vote for.

Table 5.3
Response to the Suggestion: 'It Does Not Make Much Difference Whether People Like Me Vote or Not'

Response	Kastha-danga	Baharu	Sahapur	Durgapur	Total
Agree	5 (1.71)	21 (7.04)	3 (1.0)	159 (53.0)	188 (15.79)
Partially Agree	-	80 (26.84)	4 (1.33)	-	84 (7.05)
Disagree	278 (95.20)	197 (66.10)	189 (63.0)	132 (44.0)	796 (66.89)
No Response	9 (3.08)	-	104 (34.66)	9 (3.0)	122 (10.25)
Total	292	298	300	300	1190

Table 5.4
Reasons for Voting

Reason	Kastha-danga	Baharu	Sahapur	Durgapur	Total
Persons around one pursuade one to vote	2 (0.68)	1 (0.33)	33 (11.0)	12 (4.0)	48 (4.03)
Party leader persuades me to vote	-	4 (1.34)	2 (0.66)	11 (3.66)	17 (1.42)
I feel it my duty to cast my vote	92 (31.50)	130 (43.62)	53 (17.66)	210 (70.0)	485 (40.75)
Panchayat functionaries cannot be made responsible to the people unless voters take interest in casting their votes	196 (67.12)	160 (53.69)	147 (49.0)	8 (2.66)	511 (42.94)
No Response	2 (0.68)	3 (1.0)	65 (21.66)	59 (19.66)	129 (10.84)

Autonomy in Voting Decision

In response to the question whether their voting decision was influenced by advice received from relatives, family members and friends, around eighty per cent of all respondents said 'no' (Table 5.5). The maximum number of respondents belonging to this category were, surprisingly, from Durgapur (ninety-four per cent), followed by those in Kasthadanga (eighty-five per cent). However, at least thirty per cent of the respondents in Baharu agreed that in choosing whom to vote for, they were influenced by the advice of their family, relatives, etc, in varying degrees, and about fourteen per cent of Sahapur respondents remained silent on this matter.

Similarly, on an average more than ninety per cent of the respondents denied that their voting decision was influenced by their primordial loyalties, that is, by ties of religion or caste (Table 5.6). Here the answer was more or less uniform in all the areas, except that more than ten per cent of the respondents of Sahapur were silent on the issue. This response once again confirms the fact that, in West Bengal religion and caste factors have very little impact on the outcome of elections, including panchayat elections.

Table 5.5
Extent of Voting Decision Based on the Advice of Family, Relatives, Friends etc

Response	Kastha-danga	Baharu	Sahapur	Durgapur	Total
Fully	43 (14.72)	7 (2.34)	9 (3.0)	4 (1.33)	63 (5.29)
To A Great Extent	-	5 (1.67)	17 (5.66)	1 (0.33)	23 (1.93)
To Some Extent	-	79 (26.51)	19 (6.33)	13 (4.33)	111 (9.32)
Not At All	249 (85.27)	207 (69.46)	212 (70.66)	282 (94.0)	950 (79.83)
No Response	-	-	43 ((14.33)	-	43 (3.61)
Total	292	298	300	300	1190

The findings of Tables 5.5 and 5.6 are corroborated when over eighty per cent of the respondents said that their decisions about whom to vote for were based on their own judgement (Table 5.7). There was near unanimity in the response, though around twenty-three per cent of Baharu respondents qualified this statement with a rider 'to a great extent'.

Table 5.6
Extent of Voting Decision Based on Religion or Caste Factors

Response	Kastha-danga	Baharu	Sahapur	Durgapur	Total
Fully	6 (2.05)	-	6 (2.0)	2 (0.66)	14 (1.17)
To A Great Extent	-	-	11 (3.66)	4 (1.33)	15 (1.26)
To Some Extent	-	15 (5.03)	-	7 (2.33)	22 (1.84)
Not At All	285 (97.60)	278 (93.28)	243 (81.0)	287 (95.66)	1093 (91.84)
No Response	1 (0.34)	5 (1.67)	40 (13.33)	-	46 (3.86)

Table 5.7
Response to the Question: Whether Voting Decisions of the Respondents Were Based on Their Own Judgment

Response	Kastha-danga	Baharu	Sahapur	Durgapur	Total
Fully	258 (88.35)	221 (74.16)	236 (78.66)	291 (97.0)	1006 (84.53)
To A Great Extent	-	70 (23.48)	11 (3.66)	2 (0.66)	83 (6.97)
To Some Extent	1 (.34)	3 (1.0)	22 (7.33)	6 (2.0)	32 (2.68)
Not At All	33 (11.30)	4 (1.34)	31 (10.33)	1 (0.33)	69 (5.79)

Awareness of Election Procedures

Lastly, in order to know how informed the voters were about election procedures, we attempted to assess the awareness of the respondents about the procedure for enrolment as voters, as well as the procedures for voting and counting. The result is presented in Tables 5.8, 5.9 and 5.10.

Table 5.8
Awareness of Procedure for Enrolment as Voter

Response	Kastha-danga	Baharu	Sahapur	Durgapur	Total
Aware	90 (30.82)	60 (20.13)	91 (30.33)	20 (6.66)	261 (21.93)
Not Aware	160 (54.79)	201 (67.44)	144 (48.0)	138 (46.0)	643 (54.03)
Partially Aware	42 (14.38)	37 (12.41)	65 (21.66)	142 (47.33)	286 (24.03)
Total	292	298	300	300	1190

Table 5.9
Awareness of Voting Procedure

Response	Kastha-danga	Baharu	Sahapur	Durgapur	Total
Aware	288 (98.63)	133 (44.63)	196 (65.33)	227 (75.66)	844 (70.92)
Not Aware	4 (1.36)	115 (38.59)	21 (7.0)	23 (7.66)	163 (13.69)
Partially Aware	-	50 (16.77)	42 (14.0)	40 (13.33)	132 (11.09)
No Response	-	-	41 (13.66)	10 (3.33)	51 (4.28)
Total	292	298	300	300	1190

Table 5.10
Awareness of Procedure for Counting Votes

Response	Kastha-danga	Baharu	Sahapur	Durgapur	Total
Aware	130 (44.52)	134 (44.96)	168 (56.0)	212 (70.66)	644 (54.11)
Partially Aware	10 (3.42)	-	12 (4.0)	41 (13.66)	63 (5.29)
Not Aware	152 (52.05)	111 (37.24)	120 (40)	26 (8.66)	409 (34.36)
No Response	-	53 (17.78)	-	21 (7.0)	74 (6.21)

For panchayat elections, the electoral roll used is the same prepared for assembly or parliamentary elections. Hence, the procedure for getting enrolled as voters is as prescribed by the Election Commission. It is not an easy one, as first the prospective voter has to check whether his or her name has been included during the door-to-door enumeration. If not, he or she has to fill in a form and submit it to the Electoral Registration Officer. These are not simple enough steps to encourage an ordinary villager to take the initiative. Apart from the normal bureaucratic machinery which updates the electoral rolls as per the direction of the Election Commission, the political parties also take initiative in getting at least their own supporters enlisted. Hence, a common villager may not be aware of the procedure for getting enrolled as a voter. Our data also confirms this, as it was found that on an average, more than fifty per cent of the respondents had no knowledge of the enrolment procedures (Table 5.8).

In the West Bengal Panchayat elections, the voting procedure is complicated by direct elections being held simultaneously for all the three tiers, with the voter casting his votes for all the tiers in one go.[4]

Our survey findings show that more than two-thirds of all respondents were familiar with the voting procedures (Table 5.9). An overwhelming ninety-nine per cent of Kasthadanga respondents registered positive on this point, followed by Durgapur (seventy-six per cent) and Sahapur (sixty-five per cent).

Similarly, in response to the query relating to awareness about the counting procedure, fifty-four per cent respondents said that they were aware, area-wise percentages ranging from forty-five per cent in Kasthadanga and Baharu to seventy-one per cent in Durgapur (Table 5.10). Thus most of the people are aware of the voting procedure and quite a large percentage are also familiar with the procedure for counting votes. The holding of regular panchayat elections in West Bengal, it appears, has made the rural folk quite knowledgeable about the manner of exercising their democratic rights.

Notes and References

1. Some respondents were interviewed before the election and some after the election. Hence the use of both the future and past tense in the same question.

2. Neil Webster, "Panchayati Raj in West Bengal: Popular Participation for the People or the Party?" in *Development and Change*, Sage, Vol. 23, No. 4, 1992, p. 160.

3. Kirsten Westergaard, *Peoples' Participation, Local Government and Rural Development: The Case of West Bengal, India*, Centre for Development Research, Copenhagen, 1986, p. 89.

4. Each voter is given three ballot papers – one each for the candidates for the Gram Panchayat, Panchayat Samiti and Zilla Parishad. In order to distinguish the ballot papers for each tier, ballot papers of three different colours are used. Moreover, these three ballot papers are given one by one in a particular sequence. A voter is first given a ballot paper for the GP and once he/she puts that paper in the GP ballot box after marking his/her choice, he/she is given the ballot paper for the PS and finally for the ZP.

Chapter VI

Summary and Conclusions

One of our objectives was to assess the extent to which the panchayat system has taken roots in rural West Bengal. This survey provides positive evidence to conclude that the system has taken deep roots in the socio-political life of the villagers. Today there are only a few in the village who are not aware of the panchayat or who do not know their representative in the Gram Panchayat. Most importantly, an overwhelming proportion of people (about ninety per cent) feel that the panchayat as an institution is useful and the people would suffer if the institution were to be abolished. In only one of our survey areas, namely Sahapur, respondents were found to be somewhat less enthusiastic. But here also about sixty-five per cent felt that the panchayat was a useful institution in the absence of which people would suffer.

That such a feeling of the villagers is not at a superficial level, but emanates from their life-experience, becomes apparent when we look at their answers to certain concrete questions. If the people require, respondents were asked, a handpump or want a school to be repaired or need assistance under JRY/IRDP, with whom do they place their demand? Do they approach a Government official or a political leader? The emphatic answer from all the study areas was in the negative. Nearly ninety per cent of the respondents said that in such situations, they would approach the panchayat functionary. In the case of settling village disputes nearly eighty-six per cent of the respondents would go to a panchayat leader. What is interesting is the fact that even when situations arise that threaten peace in the locality, most people (around eighty per cent) in all the study areas would like to depend on the panchayat and not on the police or magistracy who are traditional guardians of law and order. Neither settlement of village disputes nor maintenance of law and order are functions assigned to the panchayat bodies. Yet, people have found these bodies more effective (and, hence more useful) than the local executive or judicial organs of the State. These data reveal very clearly the distance that exists between the masses and the bureaucracy, exposing its lack of capacity to act as a forum of contact between the masses and the Government. It is precisely here that the panchayat is found to be more acceptable. It is therefore reasonable to suggest that the panchayats have filled a long-standing institutional gap that existed between the masses and the Government.

It has been observed that 'PRIs are dominated by economically or socially privileged sections of society and have as such facilitated the emergence of oligarchic forces yielding no benefits to weaker sections.'[1] Such oligarchic forces are usually represented by the traditional rural elite consisting of owners of substantial agricultural lands (jotedars), moneylender (mahajans) and the high caste people. In West Bengal, it is clear that this traditional rural elite has loosened its grip over the panchayat institution. Whether this has led to the dominance of the lower classes in the panchayat power-structure is a matter of debate on which divergent views have been expressed by the scholars. But what this study does confirm is the widely-held view that the traditionally dominant elite do not control the West Bengal panchayats. In all our study areas, respondents in large numbers (around eighty-six to ninety per cent) have affirmed that the domination of land owners, moneylenders and high caste people have been broken. A large majority of the respondents also expressed the view that the common people are today more conscious of their rights. These findings should not be underestimated, for they clearly indicate the presence of modernizing elements in the socio-political scene of rural West Bengal. Introduction of political panchayats and holding of regular elections to the village councils must have facilitated in fair measure such a modernization process. However, the impact of such factors as mobilization of underprivileged classes by the Left parties for gaining political control and land reform measures initiated by the United Front Government as well as the Left Front Government in breaking the dominance of traditional power structure, cannot be underestimated. In fact all these seem to have reinforced each other.

However, the institutionalization of panchayat needed something more. The grassroots democratic bodies had to be made useful to the people in order to earn credibility. This was done through the decentralisation of rural development programmes of state government through the panchayats. The beneficial effect of this policy becomes apparent when the findings of the survey show that most people believe that the panchayats have given land to the landless, improved the condition of the poor, ensured security of tenure for bargadars and adequate wage of the agricultural labourer, made substantial improvement in building infrastructure like roads or tubewells. All these benefits came either from the land reform programmes of the state government or from the poverty alleviation programmes like NREP, JRY, IRDP etc., sponsored by the central government.

The panchayats did no more than implement them. But to the common people the government is a distant and obscure entity, whereas the panchayat is near and therefore a concrete object. At the grassroots level peoples' opinion is shaped not by what happens in the state or national capital, but by what the most proximate representatives of governmental authority do. People have seen that the major decision in implementing the development programmes are being taken by the panchayats instead of the bureaucracy. Hence they give credit to these bodies for all the benefits that accrued from land reform or poverty alleviation programmes. Thus, the decentralisation of implementing responsibilities of rural development programmes through the panchayats facilitated the process of their institutionalization.

The panchayat had also been criticized for corruption, inefficiency, scant regard for procedures, political interference in day-to-day administration, 'parochial loyalties' etc., which had 'seriously limited their utility for the average villager.'[2] The scholars studying the rural politics of some states have noticed the dominance of landed gentry in the panchayat system rendering it useless for lower classes.[3] The findings of our survey on the perception of common people about the achievements of panchayats do not show these institutions in such poor light.

On the contrary, this survey as well as many other studies show that the West Bengal panchayats have handled the target-group oriented developmental or welfare programmes for rural areas with a fair measure of success. The track record of these bodies to channelise the benefits of development programmes to the poorer classes is also better than others.[4] Even the critics have found these bodies as 'more efficient and honest than in some other states.'[5] This is why West Bengal panchayats are credible institutions. Such credibility has endowed the institution with legitimacy in the eyes of the people.

What are the factors that have given the West Bengal panchayats a character different from the one depicted by the Asoka Mehta team? Part of the answer to this question has been provided by the respondents when they said that the panchayats have made people conscious of their rights. This is a reflection of the political education people could receive because of the panchayats. They have been seeing from close quarters the functioning of a democratic body endowed with substantial governmental functions. They have been participating in the elections to these bodies at regular intervals of five years wherein competing political parties would seek to enlist their support. And the issues the people would consider for formulating their views on the respective political parties are ones that are not beyond their comprehension, because panchayats have nothing to do with complex macro-problems. What could be a better ambience than this for people to educate themselves? Herein lies the strength of the democratically elected panchayat bodies. The data of our survey provide some evidence to draw such conclusions.

II

It was the fourth panchayat election which occasioned our study. The occasion was appropriate to capture peoples' response towards the periodical elections to the panchayat bodies. We had hypothesized that the people would take interest in the elections, if these institutions appeared to be relevant in their socio-economic life. Our data reveal that people attach value to these institutions and, as such, they are also expected to have a positive attitude towards the panchayat election.

The answers given to several questions by the respondents reflect such a positive attitude. Most respondents in all our study areas were aware not only of the periodicity of panchayat elections, but also of the fact that the election was due in 1993. What is more interesting is the fact that the majority of the respondents thought that it would be wrong to postpone an election which was statutorily due. Postponement of election which is statutorily due, on flimsy grounds, amounts to denial of democratic right of the elector and a politically conscious elector cannot remain complacent when this basic right is denied to him. It is, therefore, significant to notice that most of the electors of our study areas expressed that they would have been dissatisfied if the elections were not held when they were due. We do not know how strong this feeling of dissatisfaction is. For the present, it can be asserted that people have, at least, learnt to attach value to elections.

Another sign of positive attitude towards grassroots democracy is the turnout of voters at election booths. An overwhelming number of respondents have affirmed that they would, or, had cast their votes. What they said in response to our query is also confirmed by the data on the percentage of voting throughout the state (Table 7.5). In reply to our query on the sources of information about the 'date of election' or 'names of candidates', the response 'everybody was talking about it' received the highest score, indicating that the panchayat election is not the concern of political parties alone. People also have a stake in this. Excepting in places where the hold of the ruling party is absolute, election campaigning was found to be intense, complete with meetings, processions, circulation of handbills, graffitis and door-to-door canvassing. This indicates that the political parties have to strive hard for winning the confidence of voters. The voters seem to be emerging as individuals and the political control of elite factions over the masses seems to have disappeared.

Our respondents also affirmed that as voters they had autonomy in taking decisions and their decisions were not influenced by such factors as caste, religion or family ties. This is another indication of the presence of modernizing elements in rural society where primordial loyalties do not seem to influence political behaviour of the people. Even if they do, they are not at least, the determining factor in most areas.

The respondents also appeared to be quite knowledgeable about the procedure of voting or counting of votes. However, not many people know how to enrol one's name in the electoral list. It seems that in this respect they are dependent upon the normal governmental machinery which from time to time undertakes revision of the electoral roll or on political parties who take care to get the names of, at least, their supporters enrolled.

Reservation of seats for women and SC/STs was a special feature of the 1993 election. For the first time women in large numbers were to be seen in rural politics. The survey findings show that people in large majority in at least three study areas had knowledge of introduction of this novel feature. Such awareness about change being brought about in the composition of panchayats is suggestive of the interest people take in these bodies. Not only this, about half of our respondents had a positive attitude towards the provision for ensuring fair representation of women and SC/ST candidates in the panchayat bodies. People of two Gram Panchayats – Sahapur and Durgapur – are less enthusiastic about reservation, whereas, in the other two Gram Panchayats more than two-thirds of the respondents felt that it was a step in the right direction. With regard to reservation of seats for women, even in Durgapur nearly fifty per cent people were found to have a positive attitude, while in two other areas around seventy per cent had a similar attitude.

Given the inbuilt bias against women in the social as well as political life of rural areas, it would be too much to expect that the attitude reflected in the survey towards women's representation in panchayat is an indication of peoples' awareness of the problems of gender inequality and of their support to a movement for ending such inequality. However, the response at least indicates that people have generally approached the issue of women's representation in panchayat with an open mind. This is a hopeful sign. At the same time, there are still a large number of people, probably around fifty per cent, who do not find any merit in the reservation provision and some of them may even be hostile to this. Besides, the other half who seem to have approached the issue with an open mind may revise their views if the representatives of the reserved seats turn out to be dummy candidates with real leaders pulling the string from behind. Those who see in the fair representation of women and SC/STs in panchayat bodies a key to their empowerment, should realise that the battle for empowerment of the socially underprivileged has just begun with the reservation provision. Long struggles are ahead before the issue is clinched.

Our respondents claimed that they exercised their own judgement in making their voting decision. A look at the factors that influence their judgement reveals that past performance get the highest score, closely followed by such factors as policies of the party and personal qualities of the candidate. Thus, even though party affiliation is an important consideration in determining whom to vote for, the party itself has to establish its qualities of the candidates it has nominated. Among personal qualities of the candidate, honesty seems to be of prime importance, followed by sensitivity to the sufferings of the poor. Thus the variables of voting decisions of rural electors appear to be as follows:

- past performance
- policies of the party
- personal qualities of candidate: one who is honest and sensitive to the needs of the common man

Rationality in the choice of factors for taking voting decisions cannot be held in doubt. But how do the people attach value to each of these factors? Where from do they get data to make their own judgement? Our survey reveals that the mass media do not, as yet, have a significant reach in West Bengal villages and, hence their role in shaping the minds of the rural voters has so far been negligible. It is therefore safe to assume that people form their views from their personal experiences as well as from the contact with the representatives of political parties. Opportunities for evaluating candidates for Gram Panchayat are greater as compared to candidates for Panchayat Samitis and Zilla Parishad. The activities of the Gram Panchayat are more transparent, since they function right in front of the eyes of the people, whereas Panchayat Samitis and Zilla Parishads are at a distance. Therefore factors like past performance and personal qualities of candidates become stronger in respect of voting decisions for Gram Panchayats. As one moves upwards, it becomes difficult for a voter to judge a candidate as a person from his limited experiences and thus he tends to rely more on his evaluation of the political party which the candidate represents. The political parties which have wider access to the masses through their grassroots level organisations (eg. Krishak Sabha) clinch the issue in their favour. This is borne out by the pattern of voting in the Gram Panchayat, Panchayat Samiti and Zilla Parishad elections. In their bad years, the Left parties lost proportionally more seats in Gram Panchayats compared to seats lost in Panchayat Samitis and again more in Panchayat Samitis than those in Zilla Parishad (see Chapter Eight).

III

The Left parties, particularly the CPI (M) are cadre-based parties and as such have their grassroots level organisations, like 'local committees' of the party, frontal organisations such as 'Krishak Sabha'. There is a general belief that such grassroots party organisations guide and control the elected representatives in the panchayat bodies. Our survey provides indications of both positive and negative impact of such party domination over the panchayats. On the one hand, the party seems to have been careful to ensure that the panchayat leaders do not abuse their power and sincerely follow the policies of the state government. It is evident from the fact that in the two CPI(M) controlled Gram Panchayats, we found people to be most positive with regard to their perception about the usefulness of the panchayat system (Table 3.3 and 3.4). Again, when questioned on the achievements of Panchayati Raj Institutions in different spheres of rural development, generally the response from the Left party-controlled panchayats was found to be more positive compared to the Congress-controlled Gram Panchayat (Table 3.5). The beneficial effect of party's control over the functioning of panchayat both at the local level and at the upper level can also be guessed from the fact that not even one-fifth of the respondents of the opposition-led panchayats believed that justice was being denied to them (Table 3.9).

All this, however, is one side of the story. There is something more at stake. To what extent have the panchayats allowed space for common people to participate in their affairs in order to enable these institutions to express the local will? To this question we shall turn in the next section and the conclusion reached therein, as we shall see later, leaves one in doubt as to whether the imperatives of a disciplined party machinery, wedded to the principle of 'democratic centralism', are consistent with the requirements of autonomous Panchayati Raj Institutions drawing their sustenance from broad-based participation of local communities.

IV

We conceptualised panchayat not as a delivery system of higher level government, but as an institution of local self-government. The rationale of such government derives from the fact that it is capable of expressing 'local will' as distinct from the 'will' of higher level government and it provides enough room for the common people to participate in its decisions and activities. 'Local will' can find expression as the 'will' of the majority through extensive participation of common people, not of a coterie of ruling elite, in the affairs of Government. The local self-government has the capacity to allow such participation and this attribute of narrowing the gap between the ruler and the ruled, places such institutions in a different category from other types of representative government. Even though our data are limited, we have reasons to infer that the West Bengal panchayats are as yet far from achieving this goal. It also seems doubtful as to whether such a goal has, at all, been set for these institutions.

The pre-occupation of West Bengal panchayats with implementation of schemes and programmes sponsored either by the state government or the central government are fairly well known. In our survey also, the respondents were found to have given credit to the panchayats mostly for those benefits which were derived out of such schemes and programmes. But in the process of acting as the implementing agency of the state government, the panchayats seem to have become overburdened with routine work. 'Wherever we went and whichever panchayat level we met,' observed Mukarji and Bandyopadhyay, 'we were only told of activities undertaken under the Jawahar Rozgar Yojana (JRY). So pervasive is the JRY fixation that in the event of the scheme being withdrawn, the panchayats will have little to do and may have to fold up.'[6] The same thing we also noticed not only in GPs covered under this study but in panchayats of other districts also which we visited on the eve of the panchayat election. Barring a few novel experiments we came across, where people had created some community assets, pooling their own resources and labour without looking for the governmental assistance, the involvement of panchayats in JRY-related activities is so pervasive that it is apt to describe PRI as a synonym for JRY.

It should also be noted that the state government has not transferred any of its 'functions' to the panchayat bodies. What has been transferred in reality is the implementation responsibility of some schemes, especially JRY/IRDP. This has, of course, debureaucratised, to some extent, some of the state government's activities in rural development which in turn has helped the process of institutionalisation of panchayats. Our survey findings also reveal this fact. However by pegging the panchayats in routine functions, chances of realization of their potentiality to emerge as an institution of self-government have been jeopardised. As Mukarji and Bandyopadhyay had observed, the very idea of self-government was new to the panchayat leaders, 'so new that their eyes had a touch of disbelief, as they avidly took in its implications.'[7]

Short-term objectives of an organisation may overshadow its long-term objectives, if the ultimate goal remains unclear. When routinisation overtakes an organisation, 'displacement of goals' becomes an inevitability. The urgency to fulfil the target of developmental programmes handed down from above has helped the West Bengal panchayats to develop expertise in managing these programmes. This is a definite gain, for panchayat today is an efficient delivery system. But the corresponding loss is also considerable. The very process of implementing rule-bound and time-bound programmes conceived at the top has engaged the panchayats in certain routine work. As a result, its principal goal of capacity-building of the people through participation in their own development programmes seems to have been overlooked. Among our study areas, Durgapur appears to be a classic example of this.

In Durgapur, we notice a strange situation. People in this Gram Panchayat are happy with the functioning of their panchayat leaders. Everything seems to be going fine in their perception. At the same time they state that they do not have any say in what panchayat does or how it functions, and it does not matter much if people like them vote or not. Again here we find that about one-third of the people have no interest in election campaigns and another one-third have only 'slight' interest. About seventy-two per cent of the people never attended any public meetings organised by political parties and around fifty per cent are not aware, not even slightly, of the promises of the political parties (Table 4.9 to 4.11). In fact, here only three per cent of the people are found to be 'thoroughly' aware of the promises of the political parties. Again it is here that in comparison to the respondents in other three areas, the people were least aware of the important changes brought about in the composition of panchayats through reservation of seats for women and SC/STs (Table 4.15, 4.16 and 4.17). The number of persons supporting reservation as a step in right direction was found to be much lower than at least two other areas (Table 4.17).

Even though people of the area believe that their individual votes do not have much value, yet the same people said that they voted in the elections because they felt it was their 'duty' to do so. Not more than two per cent of the people of the area seem to have internalised the basic principle of democracy that elections offer an opportunity to the voter to demand accountability from the elected representatives or parties which they represent. The lack of political consciousness of Durgapur respondents becomes all the more glaring when we notice that in all the other three areas fifty per cent or more respondents assert that the panchayat functionaries cannot be made responsible to the people unless voters take interest in casting their votes, (Table 5.4). Obviously, a gap exists between the panchayat and the people. Yet, there was no fault finding with their panchayat leaders. As we have seen earlier, they are happy with the functioning of panchayats. If the panchayats have failed in any area, it is because, they feel, these bodies lack funds or do not have enough administrative power (Table 3.10).

The conclusion that we can draw from this case is that concern for achieving managerial efficiency in the Gram Panchayat has not been matched by an equal concern for participation of the people in the panchayats activities. Thus Durgapur - where the hold of CPI (M) is absolute - represents the case of a managerially efficient panchayat with very little, or no participation of people. In fact, it seems probable that the people in this area have no idea of participation at all. The relationship between the panchayat and the people of this area seems to be in the nature of benefactor-beneficiary. If this inference is correct, are we then seeing in this a syndrome of patron-client relationship in another form?

The case of Sahapur is somewhat different in that, people of this Gram Panchayat do not seem to be satisfied with the functioning of panchayats. On the achievements of the panchayat, they were less enthusiastic than others (Table 3.5). Most of them believe that lack of either funds or administrative power are not impediments before panchayats. In other words, they think that panchayats have adequate fund or administrative power. Yet, if they fail it is because panchayat functionaries do not take much interest in the well-being of the voters. They also think that there is a dearth of suitable candidates for taking control of panchayats (Table 3.10). Yet they are wise enough not to throw the 'baby' with 'bath water'. They know the distinction between the institution and the functionaries who control it. As such, we find that sixty-five per cent among them consider the panchayat institution as 'very useful' and another twenty-four per cent 'moderately useful'. Those who consider that the institution is 'not at all useful' or who have no idea about its utility constitute not more than eight per cent. (Table 3.3). Compared to others, they take more interest in election campaigns and are more aware of the promises of political parties during election (Table 4.9 & 4.11). At least sixty-three per cent of the respondents disagreed with the suggestion that 'it does not make much difference if people like me vote or not,' (Table 5.3) and one-third of the respondents said that if they are dissatisfied with the functioning of panchayats, they would express their feeling in the ballot box (Table 3.8). They did utilise the ballot box in the 1993 elections to dislodge the party which was in power during 1988-93. All these show that they have concern for panchayat institutions. Yet, these people have the feeling that common people do not have any say in what panchayats do (Table 5.2). They also feel that common people are not involved in the decision-making of panchayats (Table 3.10). Not more than two per cent of them believe that half yearly/yearly meetings of Gram Sabha are suitable for a for expressing dissatisfaction with the functioning of the panchayat (Table 3.8). Thus, the data from Sahapur suggest that unlike Durgapur, the people of this Gram Panchayat are unhappy with the manner in which panchayat is run in their area, but like Durgapur, their panchayat has also not provided any space for people to get involved in the activities of panchayat.

Hence, in both the cases there exists a gap between the panchayat and the people. In one case, people are satisfied with the functioning of the panchayat, in the other they are not. This shows that better functioning of a panchayat does not, *ipso facto*, guarantee people's participation.

It is true that in two Gram Panchayats, Kasthadanga and Baharu, most respondents disagreed with the proposition that common people do not have any say in what panchayats do. But, in a different context the same people observed that common people are not involved in the decision-making of panchayat activities. A majority of them also felt that once elected panchayat functionaries did not take much interest in the well-being of the voters. (Table 3.10). It is also necessary to take account of the fact that more than fifty-five per cent of the people of Kasthadanga and sixty-five per cent of Baharu had either 'no' interest or 'slight' interest in the election campaign of political parties and about sixty-seven per cent of Baharu were practically unaware of the promises of political parties (Table 4.9 and 4.11). Consequently, even in these two Gram Panchayats, participation of people seems to be non-existent.

Our observation regarding the lack of people's participation in panchayat becomes stronger from the uniform perception of the respondents that half-yearly and yearly meetings of the Gram Sabha are not appropriate fora for airing grievances about malfunctioning of Gram Panchayats (Table 3.8). It is clear from our study that the Gram Sabha has no significance in the West Bengal panchayat system and consequently a statutory forum which is closest in approximation to direct democracy could not be utilised effectively by the people.

V

We have seen that the panchayats have taken root in West Bengal. The process of their institutionalisation has been facilitated by the holding of regular elections to these bodies as well as by decentralisation of rural development programmes of the state government. Contrary to the belief held by some that free-play of political parties in panchayat activities would harm the village councils, the West Bengal experience shows that introduction of political panchayat has in fact, made positive contributions in the political mobilisation of people, inasmuch as political awareness of the people has increased considerably. This is reflected in the rational attitude people exhibit towards panchayat institutions in general and panchayat elections in particular. This survey also presents indications to suggest that modernising forces are in operation in West Bengal villages and political education gained through the panchayats is probably facilitating these forces.

However, implementation of certain developmental programmes, conceived and funded by higher level governments being their major responsibility, the panchayats seem to have fallen victim to the malaise of routinisation. Accent is on achieving managerial efficiency, neglecting its mobilisation function which is as important to the panchayats as its administrative functions. And it is here that the West Bengal panchayats do not seem to have come up to the expectations. If the life-blood of a panchayat is peoples' participation in its affairs, then it is necessary that ensuring peoples' involvement in panchayat activities should receive as much priority as achieving managerial efficiency in running panchayats. Data of the present study have led us to suspect that there is lack of extensive participation of people in panchayats. These institutions are, therefore, still far from realising their goal. Hence, despite their positive contribution in many spheres, the West Bengal panchayats represent a case of incomplete institutionalisation.

Notes and References

1. Government of India, *Report of the Committee on Panchayati Raj Institutions*, New Delhi, 1978, p. 6-7.

2. Ibid. p.7.

3. A brief review of the literature on the subject, especially on rural politics of Uttar Pradesh and Maharashtra, may be found in Ross Mallick, *Development Policy of a Communist Government*, Cambridge, 1993, chapter 4.

4. See Atul Kohli, *State and Poverty in India: The Politics of Reform*, Cambridge, 1987; G.K. Lieten, *Continuity and Change in Rural West Bengal*, Sage, New Delhi, 1992.

5. Ross Mallick, *op.cit.*

6. Nirmal Mukarji and D. Bandyopadhyay, *New Horizons for West Bengal's Panchayats*, Government of West Bengal, 1993, p.4.

7. Ibid. p.8.

Part Two

Chapter VII

Voter Strength and Scale of Election

I

In the 1993 panchayat elections, the total number of voters was 30 million. The corresponding number in the 1983 and 1988 elections was 20.20 million and 26.35 million respectively. 37,586 polling stations had to be set up for the 1993 election, the corresponding number in 1983 and 1988 being 28,984 and 31,771 respectively. Close to 300,000 persons were pressed into service for conducting poll of the 1993 elections. The state government had to spend around Rs.180 million for holding the election.

Reservation of Seats

There are 3,244 Gram Panchayats and 332 Panchayat Samitis in West Bengal, excluding those in the hill areas of Darjeeling district. There are sixteen Zilla Parishads and one Mahakuma Parishad. In May 1993, elections were declared for 3,223 Gram Panchayats, 328 Panchayat Samitis and sixteen Zilla Parishads, leaving out the Siliguri panchayats where five years had yet to elapse.

Table 7.1 shows the total number of seats and number of reserved/non-reserved seats in different tiers for which elections were held. Nearly sixty per cent of the Gram Panchayat seats were reserved, of which thirty-seven per cent were reserved for SC/ST candidates. SCs and STs constitute nearly thirty per cent of the total population of West Bengal. As for women, 35.22 per cent seats were reserved for them, exceeding the statutory minimum of one-third.

At the higher levels, thirty-six and thirty-five per cent seats were reserved for SC/STs in the Panchayat Samiti and Zilla Parishad respectively. Women's reservation in these tiers was thirty-five per cent. All seats taken together, there were 71,120 seats in the three tiers of which 42,051 seats (fifty-nine per cent) are reserved seats, 24,895 seats (thirty-five per cent) being reserved for women alone, including SC and ST women.

Table 7.1
Number of Seats including Reserved Seats in Each Panchayat Tier for which Elections Were Held in 1993

Tier	General Seats	Women	Reserved Seats		Total SC/ST	Total Seats	Total Seats Reserved for Women	Total Panchayat Bodies in the Tier	Average No. of seats per tier	Average No. of reserved seats for women per tier
			SC & Gen.	ST Women						
Gram Panchayat	24711 (40.50)	13553 (22.21)	14811	7936	22747 (37.28)	61011 (100.00)	21489	3223 (35.22)	19	6.67
Panchayat Samiti	4071 (43.07)	1996 (21.11)	2200	1186	3386 (35.82)	9453 (100.00)	3182	328 (33.66)	29	9.70
Zilla Parishad	287 (43.75)	142 (21.65)	145	82	227 (34.60)	656 (100.00)	224	16 (34.15)	41	14.0
Grand Total	29069	15691	17156	9204	26360	71120	24895			

Source: *Panchayati Raj*, March-April and May-June, 1993, Government of West Bengal.

Table 7.2
Party-wise Candidates for Seats in Different Tiers

(Percentages)

Tier	Total Seats	CPI (M)	CPI	FB	RSP	INC	BJP	JD & JP	IND.	Total Candidates
Gram Panchayat	61011	55906 (91.63)	3360 (5.51)	6748 (11.06)	5948 (9.74)	50982 (83.56%)	33728 (55.28)	254 (0.42)	33915 (55.59)	190841
Panchayat Samiti	9453	8738 (92.44)	480 (5.08)	1076 (11.38)	1019 (10.78)	8280 (87.59)	5824 (61.61)	48 (0.51)	5035 (53.26)	30500
Zilla Parishad	656	595 (90.70)	23 (3.51)	93 (14.18)	88 (13.41)	633 (96.49)	573 (87.35)	10 (1.52)	714 (108.84)	2729

Source: *Panchayati Raj*, May-June, 1993.
Note: CPI(M) = Communist Party of India (Marxist); CPI = Communist Party of India; FB = Forward Block; RSP = Revolutionary Socialist Party.
(These four parties, along with six other smaller parties, constitute the Left Front).
INC = Indian National Congress; BJP = Bharatiya Janata Party; JD&JP = Includes Janata Dal (A) and (B) and Janata Party; IND = Independent which includes candidates of non-recognized parties like Socialist Unity Centre of India (SUCI), Bahujan Samaj Party etc. Within such non-recognised parties, there are some smaller parties belonging to the Left Front, such as Democratic Socialist Party, Forward Block (Marxist) etc.

Table 7.3
Tier-wise Seats Won Uncontested in 1988 and 1993

Tier	Total Seats		Seats Uncontested	
	1988	1993	1988	1993
Gram Panchayat	52520	61011	4200 (7.99)	1716 (2.81)
Panchayat Samiti	9128	9453	755 (8.27)	193 (2.04)
Zilla Parishad	658	656	19 (2.88)	2 (0.30)

Source: *Panchayati Raj*, May-June, 1993
Note: Figures in brackets are percentages of uncontested seats.

Party-wise Candidates for Seats

The 1993 panchayat election saw a keen contest for seats (see Tables 7.2 and 7.3). The percentage of uncontested seats decreased in all the tiers as compared to 1988, the fall in proportion being most marked at the Samiti level. As in 1988, the proportion of uncontested seats was the lowest at the Zilla Parishad level in 1993.

Leaving aside uncontested seats, we notice that 1,89,117 candidates contested for 59,294 Gram Panchayat seats returning an average of 3.19 candidates for each seat. Similar averages for the Panchayat Samiti and Zilla Parishad work out to 3.59 and 4.17 per cent respectively.

As Table 7.2 indicates, the CPI(M), Congress and BJP were the major contesting parties in the elections. While the Left Front parties together put up candidates for all the seats in all the tiers, no other party, not even the Congress, did so. At the Gram Panchayat and Samiti levels, the latter did not contest in around seventeen per cent and thirteen per cent seats respectively. However, at the Zilla Parishad level, it contested more than ninety-six per cent seats.

Compared to the previous elections, the BJP put up a larger number of candidates, contesting over fifty per cent seats at the Gram Panchayat and eighty-seven per cent at the Zilla Parishad level. The party had not had much of a base in West Bengal. Yet it utilized the panchayat elections to make inroads in the countryside by making its presence felt everywhere.

As a single party, the CPI(M) fielded the largest number of candidates. In each tier, the party contested more than ninety per cent seats. Compared to the overwhelming presence of the CPI(M), other parties of the Left Front had to remain contented with around ten per cent seats. The CPI contested only five per cent seats at the Gram Panchayat and Samiti levels and even a lower proportion of the Zilla Parishad seats.

The four major parties of the Left Front together fielded 71,962 candidates for 61,011 Gram Panchayat seats, 11,313 candidates for 9,453 Panchayat Samiti seats and 799 candidates for 656 Zilla Parishad seats. To this may be added the candidates put up by the minor parties of the Left Front. It is evident that in nearly twenty per cent of the seats in all the tiers, the Left Front parties could not adjust seats among themselves leading to 'friendly fights'. Such 'friendly fights' among Left Front parties in panchayat elections is not new and has occurred in previous elections as well.

Reservation for and Participation of Women

Reservation of seats for women was the most novel feature of the 1993 election. How did the women respond to the opportunity given to them to be adequately represented in panchayats?

Table 7.4
Reservation for and Participation of Women Candidates in the 1993 Panchayat Election

Tier	Reserved Seats (No.)	Women Candidates (No.)	Candidate per Seat (Average)
Gram Panchayat	21489	60664	2.82
Panchayat Samiti	3182	9241	2.90
Zilla Parishad	224	873	3.89
Grand Total	24895	70778	

Source: *Panchayati Raj*, May-June, 1993.

As Table 7.4 indicates, on an average nearly three candidates contested every seat reserved for women at the Gram Panchayat and Panchayat Samiti levels with the number going up to four at the Zilla Parishad level. Out of 24,855 seats reserved for women in three tiers, only 561, or little over two per cent seats went uncontested. It would, therefore, be safe to conclude that women responded in good measure to the opportunity provided to them. In the absence of reliable figures, it is difficult to tell whether, and if so, how many women contested the general seats. From general impressions, it appears that most women candidates contested only the reserved seats.

Voter Participation

The number of votes polled as a percentage of total voters is an indication of the interest people take in elections. The figures for all the districts in this respect were not available. Table 7.5 provides information in respect of twelve of the sixteen districts.

Table 7.5
Number and Percentage of Votes Polled

District	Electorate size (in '000)	Votes Polled	Percentage (in'000)
Hooghly	1924.29	1695.97	88.13
Howrah	2077.12	1635.19	78.72
Jalpaiguri	1084.18	966.48	89.14
Birbhum	1420.62	1239.32	87.23
North Dinajpur	1018.40	863.98	84.83
Howrah	1579.81	1289.69	81.63
Murshidabad	2629.41	2324.89	88.41
Cooch Behar	1164.96	1080.1	92.71
24-Parganas (N) (except One Block)	2000.53	1729.87	86.47
Burdwan	2757.20	2244.14	81.39
24-Parganas (S)	2961.17	2571.23	86.83
Maldah	1391.54	1249.78	89.81

Source: State Panchayat Election Officer, West Bengal.

In nine out of twelve districts, more than eighty-five per cent of the voters cast their votes. In at least five districts, the percentage of votes polled was eighty-eight per cent and above, clearly indicating the extent of interest that panchayat elections generate among the rural people in the state.

II

The Position of Darjeeling District

The fourth panchayat elections were held in sixteen of the seventeen districts of West Bengal, the district left out being that of Darjeeling. The hill areas of this district (Kurseong, Kalimpong and Sadar subdivisions) are under a different kind of local administrative setup called the Darjeeling Gorkha Hill Council (DGHC) constituted under the Darjeeling Gorkha Hill Council Act, 1988. Consequently, there is no Zilla Parishad for Darjeeling district. The powers and functions of the Zilla Parishad in respect of hill subdivision district rest with the DGHC. In addition, the Council enjoys greater financial and administrative autonomy in terms of the DGHC Act. However, the law in respect of the other two tiers of the panchayat system, viz. Gram Panchayats and Panchayat Samitis, remains the same as applicable in other districts, namely the West Bengal Panchayat Act. For the plain areas of Darjeeling district, i.e. Siliguri subdivision, a special body was created by amending the state Panchayat Act in 1988. This is called Mahakuma Parishad and it enjoys all the powers and performs all the functions of a Zilla Parishad in respect of Siliguri subdivision of Darjeeling district.

In Darjeeling district no election was held when all the other West Bengal panchayats went to the polls for the third time on 28 February 1988. The postponed elections to Gram Panchayats and Panchayat Samitis and elections to the newly constituted Mahakuma Parishad in respect of Siliguri subdivision were held in 1989. But due to resistance put up by the GNLF, panchayat elections could not be held in the eighty-one Gram Panchayats and eight Panchayat Samitis of hill subdivisions of Darjeeling district. In 1994, election to the panchayats of Siliguri subdivision was held on 17 April, but it had to be restricted to the twenty-one Gram Panchayats and four Panchayat Samitis falling in Siliguri subdivision, as also to the Mahakuma Parishad of Siliguri. Once again the GNLF refused to cooperate in holding the panchayat election for the hill subdivisions. Thus, eighty-one Gram Panchayats and eight Panchayat Samitis in the hill subdivisions of Darjeeling were without any elected bodies since 1988. After a great deal of efforts, the West Bengal government had been successful in holding elections to Gram Panchayats on 26 March 1995. Election to Panchayat Samitis was not held. The newly constituted State Election Commission conducted the election, but the GNLF did not participate in this election.

III

Campaigning by Political Parties: Style and the Strategy

In West Bengal, campaigning for panchayat elections is not restricted to local issues alone. National issues are frequently raised and debated in the course of election campaigns and, indeed, national political issues, quite often, acquire pre-eminence in the panchayat election. Release of election manifestos on the eve of campaigning for the panchayat election is something unique to West Bengal and demonstrates the seriousness that political parties in the state attach to the election. It is hardly surprising, therefore, that issues like the spread of communalism, national integration and the economic liberalization programme of the central government were highlighted in the speeches of leaders belonging to various political parties as well as in the party manifestos.

While there was intense campaigning by all the political parties in the last three weeks preceding polling in practically all parts of the state, there were marked differences in the style and strategy of campaigning among the three leading players in the field, namely, the CPI(M) and Left Front, the Congress and the BJP.

As usual, the Congress party failed to act as a cohesive unit. Mamata Banerjee, the youth leader with a sizeable following, for example, preferred to remain a silent spectator in the beginning, complaining that she had not been properly consulted by Somen Mitra, the state Congress Committee president. Even the national leadership of the party appeared to have failed to respond to the situation. This was apparent from the fact that the date of the AICC session, ostensibly to discuss the issue of panchayati raj itself, coincided with polling day in West Bengal. And the West Bengal party leaders' request to change the date was met with stoic silence. Thus, in the absence of any proper direction from the state leadership, Congress party workers remained largely inactive in most parts of the state. Mr. Ghosh, a Congress Pradhan of a Gram Panchayat of Maldah district regretted that no one from the state party leadership came to campaign in his area, not even the District Congress president, whereas several BJP leaders, including the state president, and important Left Front leaders had campaigned in the area for their respective party candidates[1]. According to Mr. Ghosh, the night the panchayat election notification was broadcast on radio, cadres of CPI(M) as well as BJP covered the entire village with graffiti. They were generous enough, admitted Mr. Ghosh, to spare about one-fourth of the available space for his (Congress) party's use.

The BJP, in contrast to the Congress style of functioning, went on to utilise the fourth panchayat election as an opportunity to make its presence felt all over rural West Bengal. As noted earlier, the party fielded candidates for as many as fifty-five per cent seats in Gram Panchayats, sixty-two per cent in Panchayat Samitis and eighty-seven per cent in Zilla Parishads. In all, they fielded candidates for 40,325 seats (fifty-seven per cent) in all the three panchayat tiers. They took up the task of fighting the panchayat election in all seriousness which was reflected in the style and the strategy of their campaign.

The BJP had hardly any prior existence in the state and, therefore, virtually no organizational structure at the grassroots level. It is reported that they utilized the RSS cadres who fanned out in the villages. Their campaign, however, was limited to holding group meetings.[2] The party also involved its national leaders in the election campaign. Ms Uma Bharati, the BJP parliamentarian, visited especially the area bordering Bangladesh in order to exhort masses to give support to the BJP candidates. Other BJP national leaders, such as General Secretary, Kailashpati Mishra and some members of Parliament also campaigned. The BJP was the only party which brought leaders from outside the state to campaign for its party candidates.

It is interesting to note that probably realizing the mood of the West Bengal voters, none of these BJP leaders raised the 'mandir issue' in the course of their campaign, though they did play the 'minority card' by raising the issue of infiltration from Bangladesh in a big way. Explaining his party's position on foreign infiltrators, the state party chief is reported[3] to have said that the BJP is opposed to Bangladesh Muslim refugees only, whom they prefer to call infiltrators. At the same time he denied that the party is against Muslims since they constitute twenty-nine per cent of total voters in the state. It is also reported that the BJP fielded 1200 muslim candidates including women.[4] An interesting feature of the BJP's election campaign was the use of modern electronic media, such as video cassettes. Last-minute use of this modern electronic medium did have some impact and even Biman Bose, the Central Committee member of the CPI(M), admitted in a personal interview[5] that a section of fence-sitters among the voters was perhaps swayed by this.

Contrary to the lacklustre campaign of the Congress and aggressive electioneering by the BJP, the campaign of the CPI(M)-led Left Front was, as usual, systematic and impressive. It followed a distinct pattern in which the entire party machinery at the state, district and local levels was pressed into service according to a well-knit plan and policy, under the leadership of the towering personality of Jyoti Basu. Basu himself addressed a large number of meetings. So also did all the important leaders of the state. Even in the remotest villages, one would notice walls painted with slogans and symbols, and posters displaying the names of the Left Front candidates. For more than a month, the CPI(M)'s party newspaper, *Ganashakti*, brought out stories, features and news items highlighting the achievements of panchayati raj in West Bengal. At the village level, leaders of the party committees would hold meetings in small groups and where the situation so demanded, they would undertake door-to-door campaigns. There was also a consistency in the message that emerged through the campaign. The three issues which received prominence were: (i) achievements of panchayati raj in rural development; (ii) a vote for the Left Front would maintain the tempo of rural development and strengthen the panchayats by empowering the people; (iii) a vote for the Left Front was necessary to fight communalism as well as to challenge the dangers of the economic liberalization policies of the central government.

IV

Media Response to Panchayat Elections

Even though the mass media do not have any significant reach among the rural masses, newspapers, particularly West Bengal newspapers, seemed to have taken considerable interest in the 1993 panchayat election. Throughout the month of May and even thereafter upto the first week of June, the election was given considerable coverage in the papers in West Bengal. *Ganashakti*, the daily organ of the CPI(M), published several reports, features and stories highlighting the achievements of West Bengal panchayats and the Left Front's role in the same. *Ananda Bazar Patrika* which has the largest circulation among all language dailies in the country, also carried stories and news items almost everyday during the month of May and for a few days in June. Two other important dailies *Bartamaan* and *Aajkal*, also did the same.

Compared to the language dailies, English newspapers were less enthusiastic. The *Statesman*, an important English daily from Calcutta, however, covered the elections quite adequately. It also carried special stories on the style of campaigning, the performance of the outgoing panchayats and the prospects of different parties in individual districts. *The Telegraph*, another English daily, took a lukewarm interest in the election. Panchayats hit the paper's headlines when polling took place and results started coming in. Reports of post-poll violence in some parts of the state, particularly in Karanda village of Burdwan district, attracted the attention of all newspapers including *The Telegraph*. The Congress made it an issue for agitation and declared a *bandh* (strike) on 7 June. The press naturally had to give it coverage.

The newspapers mentioned above are all published from Calcutta and cater mainly to the urban reader. Besides the party newspaper *Ganashakti*, the other three major Bengali dailies, *Ananda Bazar Patrika*, *Aajkal* and *Bartamaan* are read by a large member of Bengalis, their combined circulation adding up to 780,915.[6] Among them, only *Bartamaan* has a special page for news relating to rural affairs.

While reporting rural events, many of these newspapers cannot overcome their urban biases. Consequently, in the coverage of panchayat elections also, the bias could not be concealed. This is evident from the type of issues covered. Generally these concentrated on the following issues: the failure of the Left Front partners in making seat adjustments among themselves; campaigning in individual districts; poll prospects of individual parties; stories on individual candidates; corruption and nepotism; party politics; violence and poll rigging; administrative arrangements of polling; poll results and analysis of performance of different parties.

The ideological slant of the newspapers were evident. The newspapers which are critical of the ruling party highlighted the negative features and those who are pro-left presented a positive picture on the above issues. The point to note is that the issues considered to be newsworthy by the various newspapers were the same, irrespective of their ideological orientation and were not different from those taken up during assembly or parliamentary elections.

That panchayats demand special coverage and attention because their functioning is not only necessary for 'good governance', but, more importantly for self-governance, is not easily evident. Hence, when newspapers choose their issues, they cannot identify the crucial aspects which have relevance for village level self-governing institutions. Probably, they search for the same qualities of good governance in the panchayats namely, efficient management and corruption-free administration, as in the governments at the Centre or state. The objective of panchayati raj is not to substitute the bureaucracy by an elected body for an efficient and corruption-free delivery system alone. The supreme value of panchayati raj lies in realizing as far as possible, what the Greeks used to call 'Demos' – a system which enables the people to participate in government and decide what is good for them.

Throughout the volumes of printed pages of five or six major newspapers, we could not come across any informed views on the relevance of the panchayat system in strengthening democracy. At the time when elections were held, the 73rd Constitution Amendment had come into being. That this Amendment has the potential to transform the polity by introducing a third stratum of government at the district, block and village levels, does not seem to have occurred to anybody. A three-part article written by an eminent civil servant[7] on this particular issue did not spark off any debate. Participation, the life-blood of the panchayat system, was a non-issue in the coverage of the 1993 panchayat election.

Another non-issue was the problem of rural poverty. Unemployment and indebtedness of the landless and marginal farmers, illiteracy, incidence of avoidable mortality are issues that seemed less newsworthy than the performance or failure of panchayat in building roads and school buildings. It was a case of looking at development in terms of physical infrastructure alone. Lack of knowledge of rural problems, issues and programmes was also found to be glaring. For example, a story published in a major Bengali daily a few days before the elections could not distinguish between 'Operation Barga' and distribution of vested land to the landless. The reporter simply overlooked the fact that the purpose of 'Operation Barga' was not to distribute vested land, but to facilitate the registration of sharecroppers so that they could ensure their legal rights.

Another important issue altogether ignored by the press was the aspect of decentralisation. At the time the panchayat election was held in 1993, eight long years had passed since decentralized planning had started in the state in 1985. There was no assessment of, not even a cursory comment on, the present status of such a decentralized system. Whether the system has succeeded or failed in introducing a 'bottom-up' approach in planning, seemed to have not merited any attention at all.

One issue which, however, received high priority in press coverage was that of reservation, particularly for women. Even though the newspapers had given due importance to this issue in their coverage, by and large, they seemed to be pessimistic about the outcome of this novel experiment. In the selection of stories, the reporter's interest in the strange spectacle of numerous village women joining the election campaign leaving their household chores was not matched by the concern for correcting the gender imbalance in the panchayats. In fact, the undercurrent of news and features on women candidates that appeared in the press was that the women would more or less act as dummies. Male chauvinism and urban biases could be noticed in the sarcastic manner in which the newsmen fashioned many of their stories.

Whatever may be the views expressed or information disseminated by the media, they make little impact on the outcome of electoral performance of political parties in panchayat elections. For, as our survey reveals, the number of rural voters who have access to newspapers is negligible. The reach of the electronic media is even less. Yet, newspapers have a role to play. They can bring to the forefront the on-going debate on decentralisation and contribute significantly in shaping public opinion, at least the opinion of urban dwellers, in favour of a decentralized polity. In a state which claims to have introduced the strongest panchayat system, the media failed to recognize the significance of the 73rd Constitution Amendment. This is a reflection of the inherent elitist and urban bias of Calcutta-based newspapers.

Notes and References

1. Personal interview, 6 June 1993.
2. *The Statesman*, Calcutta, 23 May 1993.
3. Ibid, 29 May 1993.
4. Ibid, 12 June 1993.
5. Interview at State Party Headquarters, Calcutta, 10 June 1993.
6. See, *INS Press Hand Book*, 1994.
7. Nirmal Mukarji, "Third Stratum", in *The Statesman*, Calcutta, 11-13 May 1993.

Chapter VIII

Performance of Different Political Parties

The CPI(M) and its partners in the Left Front have been dominating the West Bengal panchayats since 1978. The CPI(M), as the single largest party has, in fact, been in the driver's seat. The main opposition has come from the Congress, but even at the best of times, this party could not get more than thirty-two per cent of the seats in Gram Panchayats. The seats obtained by this party in Panchayat Samitis and Zilla Parishads was even less.

In order to appreciate the comparative performance of different parties over the last four elections, we may have a look at Table 8.1(A), (B) and (C). Some of the interesting features that emerge are as follows:

The performance of individual parties follows a zig-zag course. Starting from 1978, the CPI(M) and the Left parties witnessed good performance (in terms of percentage of seats bagged by them) followed by poor performance, which in turn was followed again by good performance. The Congress also met the same fate with the difference that good time of the Left has been its bad time.

The CPI(M)'s share in Gram Panchayat seats was sixty per cent, fifty-three per cent, sixty-four per cent and fifty-eight per cent, in the 1978, 1983, 1988 and 1993 elections respectively (Table 8.1[A]). Corresponding figures for Congress were ten per cent, thirty-two per cent, twenty-three per cent and twenty-seven per cent. The same pattern emerged in Panchayat Samiti and Zilla Parishad seats also.

The CPI(M) has consistently maintained its lead, but its share of seats improves as it moves from Gram Panchayat to Panchayat Samiti and then to Zilla Parishad. In Gram Panchayats, its hold has been around sixty per cent seats, the range of variation being fifty-three per cent in 1983 to sixty-four per cent in 1988. In Panchayat Samitis (Table 8.1[B]), the average is more than sixty-five per cent and in Zilla Parishads (Table 8.1[C]), as high as seventy-five per cent to eighty per cent. Even in its worst time i.e., in 1983, it occupied sixty-seven per cent of Zilla Parishad seats.

For looking at the performance figures from another angle, we may try to make three sets of comparisons – one between 1978 and 1983, another between 1983 and 1988 and finally between 1988 and 1993. The first and third elections were good for the CPI(M) and the Left. The opposition fared better in the other two.

An analysis of Tables 8.2, 8.3 and 8.4 indicates, that the best year for the Opposition was 1983 when it gained more than twenty-two per cent of the seats in the two lower tiers and around twenty per cent in Zilla Parishads. But this gain was mostly at the expense of Independent candidates and smaller parties, while the CPI(M) could restrict its loss within seven to eight per cent of the seats (Table 8.2). On the other hand, in 1988, the ruling Left Front gained ground as compared to the 1983 election mainly at the expense of the Congress party, followed by Independents and other smaller parties. As is clear from Table 8.3, the CPI(M) secured eleven per cent more seats in 1988 at the Gram Panchayat level, improving its position further from its 1978 position, since it had lost seven per cent seats in 1983 as compared to 1978. The other constituents of the Left Front like the FB, the RSP and the CPI were also gainers but their gains were insignificant. The trend, we find, is rather steady, slightly increasing at the Panchayat Samiti and Zilla Parishad levels, all at the cost of the Congress and Independents and others.

In 1993, the Left Front lost eight per cent of the seats at the Gram Panchayat level, of which the CPI(M)'s share was six per cent (Table 8.4). In Panchayat Samitis, the loss of seats for the CPI(M) was smaller, around five per cent, and in Zilla Parishads the party's loss was virtually negligible, being less than one per cent. Among the winners, the gains were equally shared by the Congress and the BJP in Gram Panchayats. But the BJP's limited success in Gram Panchayats could not be maintained in upper tiers of panchayats. In Zilla Parishads, the BJP could not win even a single seat.

It has been commented, and rightly so, that it is in Gram Panchayats that some inroads can be made by the Opposition in the citadel of the ruling Left Front. It has also been observed that at the Gram Parishad level, administration is transparent and here people are not always swayed by the party network. They can judge the candidates in terms of their individual merit because they can see their performance from close quarters and can vote according to their own judgement. As one moves up, administration becomes more opaque and, accordingly, at the higher levels people have to choose a candidate belonging to the party they support. This is the reason, according to some, for the position of the CPI(M) getting stronger from the Gram Panchayat level to the Panchayat Samiti level, and being absolute in the Zilla Parishads.

That apart, what could be the other possible factors leading to the uneven course of relative gains and losses of the main political parties in alternate panchayat elections? It appears that the corresponding performance of both these parties in successive panchayat elections is, to some extent, in tune with the corresponding position of the Congress and the Opposition, including the CPI(M), at the centrestage of national politics in the country. And this is hardly surprising. For, as noted earlier, since 1978 panchayat elections in West Bengal have been fought in the backdrop of the national political scene.

It may be recalled here that during the first election held in 1978 when the West Bengal political scene was agog with the historic decision of the Left Front to bring political parties in the panchayat arena, the Congress was yet to recover from the shock of its humiliating defeat at the Centre. The party was literally in shambles, at least in the northern Indian states, and its West Bengal unit was tottering.

By the time the second panchayat election was held in 1983, the Congress was back in power in Delhi and barring West Bengal, the party had also regained power in most of the north Indian states. Correspondingly, in West Bengal panchayats, the party could increase its seats by three times in Gram Panchayats (Table 8.1[A]), four times in Panchayat Samitis (Table 8.1[B]) and as much as nearly seven times in Zilla Parishads (Table 8.1 [C]). Without minimising the impact of other factors, it would perhaps not be unrealistic to infer that better fortune for the Congress in the national political scene of 1983 had its bearing on the course of events in the state panchayat elections.

The effect of the twist in national politics is seemingly once again visible in the third panchayat election. The Congress party, it may be recalled, was then under cloud mainly because of the Bofors issue and it was difficult for the party to muster enough will and energy to fight with the Left Front at the West Bengal hustings on the same footing. Table 8.3 reveals nearly nine per cent loss in 1988 at the Gram Panchayat level for the Congress-I, whereas the CPI(M) was found to be improving its gains by eleven per cent. Loss of seats for Congress in Panchayat Samiti and Zilla Parishad was even more, being eleven per cent in the former and nearly fourteen per cent in the latter.

The results of 1993 elections show again the CPI(M) being a loser in comparison to its 1988 electoral victory – by a margin of nearly seven per cent of the total seats in Gram Panchayats and about five per cent in Panchayat Samitis. On the other hand, the Congress gained three and four per cent more seats in Gram Panchayats and Panchayat Samitis respectively than what it had obtained in the 1988 elections (Table 8.4). But what is important to note in the fourth panchayat election is the emergence of the BJP almost from nowhere. From only thirty-two seats in Gram Panchayats and three seats in Panchayat Samitis in 1988, the party managed to capture 2,767 seats in Gram Panchayats and 125 seats in Panchayat Samitis (Tables 8.1[A] and 8.1[B]). Even though percentage-wise, the performance of BJP was not impressive (four per cent of total Gram Panchayat seats and three per cent of total Panchayat Samiti seats), gain for the party in terms of number of seats captured in Gram Panchayats and Panchayat Samitis in 1993, was a quantum jump indeed. Moreover, one cannot overlook the fact that the BJP's share of seats in Gram Panchayats is much more than all the constituents of Left Front other than the CPI(M). Even in Panchayat Samitis, its performance is impressive compared to parties like the Forward Bloc or the CPI. Such a sudden rise for the BJP in the West Bengal rural scene has to be explained by its performance in national politics after the 1989 and 1991 parliamentary elections and more particularly after the 1991 Assembly elections in which it formed governments in as many as four states. Thus the emergence of the BJP from nowhere in West Bengal panchayats of 1993, is again in correspondence with our proposition that the national political scene has a bearing upon the panchayat elections in the state.

Table 8.1
Performance of Political Parties in Four Panchayat Elections held between 1978 and 1993
A - GRAM PANCHAYAT

Year	Seats	CPI (M)	FB	RSP	CPI	Congress	Cong (R)	Janata	BJP	Ind. & other Parties
1978	46401	28105 (60.57)	1539 (3.31)	1674 (3.61)	825 (1.78)	4536 (9.77)	580 (1.25)	5 (0.01)		9137 (19.69)
1983	45675	24410 (53.44)	1084 (2.37)	1241 (2.72)	716 (1.57)	14733 (32.26)	-	44 (0.10)	34 (0.07)	3413 (7.47)
1988	52473	33834 (64.48)	1398 (2.66)	1581 (3.01)	907 (1.73)	12239 (23.33)	-	21 (0.04)	32 (0.06)	2461 (4.69)
1993	60965	35342 (57.97)	1233 (2.03)	1526 (2.50)	799 (1.31)	16292 (26.73)	-	17 (0.03)	2367 (3.88)	3384 (5.55)

B - PANCHAYAT SAMITI

Year	Seats	CPI (M)	FB	RSP	CPI	Congress	Cong (R)	Janata	BJP	Ind. & other Parties
1978	8483	5596 (65.96)	320 (3.77)	393 (4.63)	132 (1.55)	623 (7.34)	105 (1.23)	2 (0.02)	-	1312 (15.46)
1983	8591	5050 (58.78)	194 (2.26)	248 (2.89)	97 (1.13)	2543 (29.60)	-	11 (0.13)	2 (0.02)	446 (5.19)
1988	9116	6550 (71.85)	227 (2.49)	276 (3.03)	117 (1.28)	1687 (18.51)	-	3 (0.03)	3 (0.03)	253 (2.78)
1993	9446	6333 (67.04)	169 (1.79)	241 (2.55)	90 (0.95)	2158 (22.84)	-	-	125 (1.32)	330 (3.49)

C - ZILLA PARISHAD

Year	Seats	CPI (M)	FB	RSP	CPI	Congress	Cong (R)	Janata	BJP	Ind. & other Parties
1978	645	488 (75.66)	44 (6.82)	30 (4.65)	5 (0.77)	23 (3.57)	4 (0.62)	-	-	51 (7.90)
1983	637	429 (67.35)	25 (3.92)	14 (2.20)	-	149 (23.39)	-	-	-	20 (3.14)
1988	657	531 (80.82)	22 (3.35)	25 (3.80)	7 (1.06)	62 (9.43)	-	-	-	10 (1.52)
1993	655	528 (80.61)	17 (2.60)	14 (2.14)	6 (0.92)	73 (11.14)	-	-	-	17 (2.59)

Source: *Panchayati Raj*, May-June, 1993.

Table 8.2
Gains and Losses of Parties in 1983 Election Compared to Their Performance in 1978 Election

Tier	Gain (per cent seats) in 1983				Loss (per cent seats) in 1983					
	Congress	BJP	Others	Total	CPI (M)	FB	RSP	CPI	Cong (R) Ind. & Others	Total
GP	22.49	0.07	0.09	22.65	7.13	0.94	0.89	0.21	13.47	22.64
PS	22.22	0.02	0.11	22.35	7.5	1.53	1.3	0.43	11.59	22.35
ZP	19.82	-	-	19.82	8.31	2.9	2.45	0.77	5.38	19.82

Note: GP - Gram Panchayat, PS - Panchayat Samiti, ZP - Zilla Parishad

Table 8.3
Gains and Losses of Political Parties in 1988 Elections as Compared to Their Performance in 1983 Election

Tier	CPI (M)	FB	RSP	CPI	Total	BJP	Congress	Janata	BJP	FB	Ind. & Other Parties	Total
GP	11.04	0.29	0.29	0.16	11.78	-	8.93	0.06	0.01	-	2.78	11.78
PS	13.07	0.23	0.14	0.15	13.60	0.01	11.09	0.10	-	-	2.41	13.60
ZP	13.47	-	1.61	1.07*	16.15	13.96	-	-	1.62	0.57*	16.15	

Note: GP - Gram Panchayat, PS - Panchayat Samiti, ZP - Zilla Panchayat

* CPI failed to win even a single seat at the ZP level in 1983, though it had won 0.77 per cent seats (five) in 1978.

* FB's gain in 1988 election was limited to GP and PS level only as it lost 0.57 per cent of the seats in ZP, though both loss and gain was almost negligible, being less than one per cent in either case.

Table 8.4
Gains and Losses of Political Parties in 1993 Elections as Compared to Their Performance in 1988

	Gain (per cent of seats) in 1993				Loss (per cent of seats) in 1993				
Tier	Congress	BJP	Others	Total	CPI(M)	FB	RSP	CPI	Total
GP	3.40	3.82	0.86	8.08	6.51	0.63	0.51	0.42	8.07
PS	4.34	1.29	0.71	6.34	4.81	0.70	0.48	0.33	6.32
ZP	1.71		1.07	2.78	0.21	0.75	1.67	0.15	2.78

Note: GP - Gram Panchayat, PS - Panchayat Samiti, ZP - Zilla Panchayat

Index